Improving Your Teaching Skills:
A Guide for Student Teachers and Practitioners

B. Ann Boyce, PhD
Teacher Education in Health & Physical Education
Program Area of Kinesiology

Boston Burr Ridge, IL Dubuque, IA Madison, WI New York
San Francisco St. Louis Bangkok Bogotá Caracas Kuala Lumpur
Lisbon London Madrid Mexico City Milan Montreal New Delhi
Santiago Seoul Singapore Sydney Taipei Toronto

The *McGraw-Hill* Companies

Mc Graw Hill **Higher Education**

Improving Your Teaching Skills:
A Guide for Student Teachers and Practitioners, First Edition
B. Ann Boyce, PhD

ISBN 0-07-284128-1

www.mhhe.com

Table of Contents

Dedication

Throughout life there are many individuals who significantly shape both our thinking and our aspirations. This book is dedicated to those who have helped me grow and develop.

My mom and dad, who always believed in me and gave me wings to aid in the attainment of my dreams. My dad, who took me fishing and taught me to shoot a rifle and drive a car, was always supportive, and while our dinner conversations were not always good for the digestion, they taught me the importance of a well-framed argument. My mother's gallant fight with cancer has taught me courage and persistence and allowed me to know her on a new level beyond that of parent and child, but now as friend and confidant.

My good friend and colleague, Linda Bunker, who mentored me throughout my career at Virginia, is one of the most amazing individuals I have ever met. Her work ethic and professionalism stand as a testament to all who know her. She also fights the good fight with tenacity, intelligence, dignity and hope.

Lastly, Professor Janet Wells, my major professor who once told me that I was at a turning point in my professional career and if I did not take the next step that she would help me do so. When I think of her, I think of her strength of character, her professionalism and her abiding faith in me.

Preface

In order for teachers at all levels (student teachers, beginning teachers, experienced teachers) to be effective, they must design and implement educational environments that facilitate student learning. Many teacher behaviors are associated with effective teaching and most pedagogists agree that effective teachers create structured learning environments that promote mastery of motor skills and attainment of physical fitness while optimizing student success (Berliner, 1984; Gage, 1984; Medely, 1977; Rink, 1985, 1996; Rosenshine, 1983; Siedentop & Tannehill, 2000). While this may seem simple to the uninitiated, the pedagogical/teaching skills required to become an effective teacher are complex and multi-faceted, yet they are also attainable.

Improving Your Teaching Skills: A Guide for Student Teachers and Practitioners was constructed to familiarize teachers with the fundamental tenets of effective teaching. This practical guide covers many of the skills that are used by effective teachers, and associated with the research on teacher effectiveness, observation tools that measure these skills, performance standards related to skill attainment and strategies that assist in the development of effective teaching practices for student teachers and practitioners, alike. This is accomplished through the implementation of a goal-setting model, which uses systematic observation to address specific teaching behaviors. These behaviors are introduced in a sequential manner, permitting teachers to focus on individual pedagogical behaviors that can increase their effectiveness. The observation tools focus on specific behaviors and are designed for use by student teachers (ST) and their respective cooperating teachers (CT), as well as practicing teachers (PT). These tools focus on single teacher behaviors and require a minimum amount of training for use in K-12 school settings. Even though the tools are targeted to single behaviors, it is important to note that many teacher behaviors (e.g., practice, management and instructional episodes) are interlinked. It was beyond the scope of this book to have teachers (ST/CT and PT) collect multi-faceted information on interlinking teacher behaviors because the resulting tools would be too cumbersome for teacher use. However, the application of these tools which focus on signal behaviors and the subsequent information gleaned from them will provide valuable information to objectively analyze teaching skills and track progress toward being a more effective educator.

This book is organized in a hierarchical manner: addressing teacher behaviors in a sequential order that may naturally emerge as teaching skills develop. The first section focuses on the establishment of a structured learning environment through class and behavior management techniques. From research on teacher effectiveness, we know that teaching cannot proceed until an appropriate learning environment has been established (Doyle, 1979; Rink, 1993; Siedentop & Tannehill, 2000; Soar & Soar, 1979). The second section addresses the practice of motor skills and/or participation in fitness activities by students. The practice of skills is the most important variable controlling the learning of motor skills (Schmidt & Wrisberg, 2000). In addition, students cannot become physically fit unless they participate in fitness activities at the proper levels of intensity, frequency and duration (US Department of Health & Human Services, 1996). The final section addresses student learning in terms of successful practice and/or successful participation in fitness activities. Student success is the hallmark of an effective teacher and it is the standard for judging a teacher's true effectiveness.

It is important to acknowledge the work of previous educational researchers and pedagogists (e.g., Anderson & Barrette, 1978; Berliner, 1984; Brophy & Good, 1986; Gage, 1984; Graham, Holt/Hale, & Parker, 2001; Medely, 1977; Rink, 1985, 1996; Rosenshine, 1983; Siedentop, 1983; Siedentop & Tannehill, 2000) who have laid the foundation for this manuscript. A tremendous amount of research on teacher effectiveness was conducted in the 1970s and 1980s and much of what we know about this subject is the result of this early work. In addition, several pedagogists (e.g., Metzler, 1990; Randall, 1992) have developed procedures for supervision in physical education that have greatly contributed to what we know about the assessment of effective teaching through systematic observation techniques. Lastly, the research on goal setting has been pioneered through the work of Edwin Locke and his colleagues (Locke & Latham, 1990). All of these individuals in their respective fields have contributed to the ideas and production of this manuscript.

Lastly, I would like to acknowledge the contributions of practicing teachers from Northern Virginia, cooperating teachers in Albemarle County, and student teachers from the University of Virginia, who helped field test the tasks found in this manuscript. Their constructive feedback kept me grounded in the real world and was critical in revision process.

Note to the Student Teacher (ST) and Cooperating Teacher (CT)

The student teaching experience is the culmination of your training in teacher education. In many cases this experience will help you clearly define yourself as a physical educator. The pedagogical/teaching and professional skills that you develop during this experience will serve as your foundation when you enter the teaching profession. While this experience is a source of great anxiety, it is also a time of exploration and discovery when you can apply and begin to evaluate all of the concepts and strategies to which you were introduced during your teacher education program.

The relationship that you develop with your cooperating teacher (CT) is critical. This individual will guide you through your student teaching experience on a daily basis. Since the development of your teaching skills is a progressive journey, you should rely on your CT's experience and expertise to provide you with relevant feedback on your emerging teaching skills. Viewing your CT as your mentor or coach will help you develop a strong relationship that can be mutually beneficial. However, this relationship is not a one-way street. The CT can expect you to bring enthusiasm, expertise in content areas, new teaching strategies, instructional styles, ideas and resources for improving their existing program. Hard work, perseverance, flexibility and the ability to learn from constructive feedback are all expectations of student teaching.

Improving Your Teaching Skills: A Guide for Student Teachers and Practitioners is designed to lead you and your CT through the basic tenets of effective teaching. This book is divided into three major sections: (a) establishing structure and class management, (b) creating practice opportunities for your students and (c) ensuring student success. The 14 tasks, or subsections, address specific teaching behaviors and can be utilized on a weekly or bi-weekly basis to help you make improvements in your teaching skills.

Performance standards are also introduced to help you and your CT assess your teaching skills. There are two levels of performance standards found within this book. The first level of standards functions as a general guideline and can be located within the task example's section (see Step 3 under Long and Short Term Goals in tasks 2- 6 and 11 -13). The second level of standards has been taken from the literature on teacher effectiveness and these standards are strongly suggested for use and appear in bold type under the heading entitled **Beginning Teacher Performance Standards (BTPS)** and can be located in Step 3 under Long Term Goals for tasks 7-11 and 14. While these standards are for the most part achievable, sometimes standards will need to be adjusted for the context of your teaching situation. For example, context variables such as large class sizes, limited equipment and facilitates are factors that can affect teachers. Strategies for improving your effectiveness, as well as a goal setting model, are provided to help you attain your full potential as a beginning teacher.

A goal-setting model is provided to help you and your CT assess your current level of performance and plan for future improvements. Briefly, the goal setting process will consist of seven steps:

Step 1- Identification of a teaching behavior (e.g., feedback to students)

Step 2- Collection of baseline data on that behavior

Step 3- Setting a specific long-term goal (LTG) and short-term goals (STGs) related to that behavior (in some cases [see tasks 7-11 and 14], a Beginning Teacher Performance Standards [BTPS] for success will also be provided to help you set the LTG—this will appear in bold type; the remaining standards are provided as general guidelines)

Step 4 - Identification and use of strategies that will help you attain your goal

Step 5 - Throughout the week, collection of data to check on your progress (your CT can help you do this) and comparison of this information to your STGs and LTG

Step 6- At the end of the week, collection of post test data on your designated behavior and comparison of post test data to your LTG to see if you achieved it

Step 7 - Revision of the goal setting process, if you did not achieve your goal

This goal setting model was adapted from Boyce & King, (1993). The pivotal parts of the goal setting process are: (a) the setting of specific and measurable goal, (b) the construction of strategies to help you attain your goal and (c) the on going monitoring of your progress to check for improvements.

Note to the University Supervisor (US)

Student teaching is the culminating experience for your majors in teacher education. It is a time when they leave their institutions of higher learning, enter the real world of teaching and begin to define themselves as future physical educators. Much of what you have tried to teach them about teaching and teacher effectiveness will be put to the test during this experience. For the most part, they will practice their teaching skills without the benefit of the University Supervisor's guidance. University Supervisors (US) can best serve their Student Teachers (ST) through school visitations and reflective opportunities to learn from their teaching experiences. During school visitations, you can: (a) observe teaching episodes, (b) collect information on the ST's performance, (c) debrief the ST on their own observations as well as those of the Cooperating Teacher (CT), (d) identify area(s) where improvements are needed and (e) outline strategies and set goals that address the areas of potential improvements.

However, the fact remains, the CT will have the most influence on the ST's progress during this field experience. Therefore, it is imperative to gain the CT's support when instituting a systematic teacher observation system, especially when the CT will be the one collecting this information and using it to help modify the teaching behavior of their ST. While the instruments presented in this book are easy to use, the US may need to provide the CT with some assistance while learning to use these tools. This task can be accomplished in several ways. The US can train the STs during the seminar and they can in turn, train their respective CTs, or the US can directly train the CTs. With a limited amount of in-service (provided to the CT) or in-class (provided to the ST) training, the CT and ST can quickly master these observation and data collection skills. Systematically using these instruments during your field visits and then sharing the results with the CT and ST can further enhance this learning process. Another way to help STs is to introduce the tenets of teacher effectiveness and the instruments that measure those behaviors during your methods courses. Students can complete a "Self-Improvement Project" which utilizes selected instruments/tasks found in this book. This process exposes them to the use of systematic observation and a model of goal setting on a limited scale. These same students can fully implement this process during their students' teaching experience. In many cases, even without this additional help, the CT and ST can simply read the instructions in the book, including the examples, provided and complete the tasks relative to specific teaching behaviors.

Beginning Teacher Performance Standards (BTPS), in the form of suggested "long term goals," are given for selected tasks and these criteria are based on Medley's (1977) work with beginning teachers, an internal university document based on Medley's work (University of Virginia's Elementary BTAP Standards, 1989), Rosenshine's (1983) recommendation regarding student success rates, as well as the work of pedagogists within physical education (Rink, 1996; Siedentop, 1991). These suggested BTPS can be found in the task example section – Step 3 under Long Term Goals (see tasks 7 –11 and 14) with remaining standards intended as general guidelines (see the LTG & STGs in tasks 2-6 and 12-13 in the same section).

These BTPS have been used successfully with the physical education majors at the University of Virginia for over ten years. While these BTPS are not easily achieved, they do provide realistic expectations for STs related to specific teacher behaviors. However, sometimes standards may need to be modified based on the context of the school, so you should feel free to modify these standards to reflect your philosophy and expectations. In addition, strategies for attaining the performance criteria (long and short term goals) have been field tested, and are provided within the framework of a goal setting model that can help your student teachers refine their teaching skills.

This book is intended to function as a guide for the development of an ST's teaching skills. Student teachers enter this culminating experience with a variety of skills. Some students already possess effective behavior and class management skills and should focus on providing successful practice opportunities for their pupils. Other STs need to practice effective behavior and class management techniques before they can successfully teach content. Therefore, flexibility is needed when deciding on the areas/tasks of teacher effectiveness on which to focus. This book contains a "Trouble Shooting Chart" that can help the ST, CT and US decide which tasks to focus on in order to improve the ST's effectiveness.

Note to the Practicing Teacher (PT)

The practice and improvement of teaching is an ongoing process that leads many teachers to examine their existing pedagogical skills and make changes where necessary. *Improving Your Teaching Skills: A Guide for Student Teachers and Practitioners* is designed to direct you through the tenets of effective teaching. It is divided into three major sections: (a) establishing structure and class management, (b) creating practice opportunities for your students and (c) ensuring student success. The 14 tasks, or subsections, address specific teaching behaviors and can be utilized to help you make improvements in your teaching skills. In addition, many of the performance standards cited in this book can be used as benchmarks, as they represent standards for effective beginning teachers (see task example section – Step 3 under Long Term Goals, with the standards identified as **Beginning Teacher Performance Standards [BTPS]** under tasks 7-11 and 14). While these standards are achievable, under certain circumstances they may need to be modified to account for the contextual considerations (e.g., large class size, limited equipment and facilities, SES level of students) present in your school. The information gathered from the tasks in this book can be used as a part of your teaching portfolio. It will provide evidence of your continuing commitment to the improvement of your teaching skills.

You can complete many of the tasks in this book without assistance by using a stopwatch, tape and/or video recorder to note your performance on selected tasks. However, some of the tasks will require the cooperation of a colleague to gather the needed information. This process could be completed jointly with teachers functioning as partners. Directions for solo or partner data collection can be found in each task under Steps 1 and 2. The designators, PT and/or partners (P), located in steps 1 and 2 are in bold type. The same data gathering process applies to the collection of weekly and post test data sessions.

This book is intended to function as a handbook for the development of teaching skills. Effective teachers utilize a wide variety of pedagogical skills. Many teachers already possess effective behavior and class management skills and should therefore focus on providing successful practice opportunities for their students. This book contains a **Trouble Shooting Chart** that can help you decide on the tasks that can best help improve your teaching skills.

A goal setting model will help you assess your current level of performance and plan for future improvements (goal setting model was adapted from Boyce & King, 1993). Briefly, the goal setting process will consist of seven steps:

Step 1- Identification of a teaching behavior (e.g., feedback to students)
Step 2- Collection of baseline data on that behavior
Step 3- Setting a specific long-term goal (LTG) and short-term goals (STGs) related to that behavior (in some cases [see tasks 7-11 and 14], a Beginning Teacher Performance Standards [BTPS] for success will also be provided to help

you set the LTG—this will appear in bold type; the remaining standards are provided as general guidelines)
<u>Step 4</u> - Identification and use of strategies that will help you attain your goal
<u>Step 5</u> – Collection of data to check on your progress via comparison of this information to your STGs and LTG.
<u>Step 6</u>- Collection of post test data on your designated behavior and comparison of this data to your LTG to see if you achieved your LTG
<u>Step 7</u> - Revision of the goal setting process, if you did not achieve your goal

The good news is that teaching is a skill that can be learned, modified and improved upon (Metzler, 1990). All it takes is the time and commitment to the process of monitoring your teaching practices and making changes (e.g., adopting new teaching strategies) in order to become a more effective teacher.

Trouble Shooting Chart for Student Teachers (ST)

This chart will help Student Teachers (STs) and Cooperating Teachers (CTs) identify areas of concern related to the ST's teaching performance. Questions focus on areas of concern and the corresponding tasks are listed to help the STs assess and address those areas.

QUESTION	TASK
Behavior and Class Management:	
What management strategies does my CT use?	Task 1
Do I deal quickly and effectively with inappropriate student behavior?	Task 2
Do my students take too long to comply with my requests?	Task 3
Are my students "on-task" throughout the lesson?	Task 4
Do I keep my "Back to the Wall" throughout the lesson?	Task 5
Is the environment I create in my gymnasium a positive one?	Task 6
How much time do I spend on management?	Task 7
Student Practice:	
Are my students receiving adequate and appropriate feedback?	Task 8
Do I talk too much?	Task 9
Are my students spending too much time waiting?	Task 10
How much opportunity for practice do my students receive?	Task 11
Student Practice with Success:	
Do I **plan** extensions on tasks, refinements—cues and challenges that account for individual differences (motor – precontrol, control, … or students with special needs) in my lesson plan?	Task 12
Do I **implement** extensions, refinements and challenges that account for individual differences (motor – precontrol, control, … or students with special needs) in actual lessons, while I teach?	Task 13
Do all of my students receive the same practice opportunity and are they successful approximately 80% of the time?	Task 14

Trouble Shooting Chart for Practicing Teachers (PT)

This chart will help Practicing Teachers (PTs) identify areas of needed improvement related to their teaching performance. Questions focus on areas of needed improvement, and the corresponding tasks are listed to help the PTs assess and address those areas.

QUESTION	TASK
Behavior and Class Management:	
What management strategies do I use?	Task 1
Do I deal quickly and effectively with inappropriate student behavior?	Task 2
Do my students take too long to comply with my requests?	Task 3
Are my students "on-task" throughout the lesson?	Task 4
Do I keep my "Back to the Wall" throughout the lesson?	Task 5
Is the environment I create in my gymnasium a positive one?	Task 6
How much time do I spend on management?	Task 7
Student Practice:	
Are my students receiving adequate and appropriate feedback?	Task 8
Do I talk too much?	Task 9
Are my students spending too much time waiting?	Task 10
How much opportunity for practice do my students receive?	Task 11
Student Practice with Success:	
Do I **plan** extensions on tasks, refinements—cues and challenges that account for individual differences (motor – precontrol, control, … or students with special needs) in my lesson plan?	Task 12
Do I **implement** extensions, refinements and challenges that account for individual differences (motor – precontrol, control, … or students with special needs) in actual lessons, while I teach?	Task 13
Do all of my students receive the same practice opportunity and are they successful approximately 80% of the time?	Task 14

Part One

Behavior & Class Management:

Creating a Structured Learning Environment

TASK 1
Inventory of Behavior & Class Management Techniques

Teachers regard student misbehavior as a major obstacle to their teaching success (Swick, 1981). One proactive way to deal with the many challenges associated with this problem is through the implementation of effective behavior and classroom management strategies. Students rely on their teachers to establish classroom rules and policies so they know what is expected of them when they come to class. Planning is the key to good classroom management. Students need to practice and receive feedback on class routines (roll call, getting student attention, etc.).

As a student teacher (**ST**), you need to be aware of the rules and policies already established by your cooperating teacher (**CT**) as well as their school and school system. It is imperative that you know how your CT would handle specific behavior and class management issues so that you can deal with these dilemmas in a similar manner. The *Inventory of Behavior & Class Management Techniques* Worksheet found on the next few pages will give you the opportunity to discuss and record your CT's recommendations related to specific behavior issues as well as classroom management rules and policies. In some cases, your school or school system will have pre-established policies for dealing with certain behavior issues (e.g., policy related to drug or alcohol use). This inventory should be completed during the pre-planning period in order to give you the opportunity to discuss these issues prior to the arrival of the students. Take advantage of your CT's knowledge and experience in this area and use this opportunity to acquaint yourself with the CT's and your school's expectations regarding behavior and classroom management.

As a practicing teacher (**PT**), it is important that you plan how you will handle class and behavior management issues so that when behavioral issues arise, you will be prepared to react to them in a fair and consistent manner. The *Inventory of Behavior & Class Management Techniques* Worksheet found on the following pages will give you the opportunity to think about and record your recommendations related to specific behavior issues as well as classroom management rules and policies. In some cases, your school or school system may have pre-established policies for dealing with certain behavior issues (e.g., policy related to drug or alcohol use). This self-evaluation inventory should be completed during your pre-planning week and this will give you the opportunity to decide on these issues prior to the arrival of the students. Try to anticipate areas (e.g., effect of fire drills on your class) where problems may arise so that you can be ready to deal with these issues.

Remember that effective teachers spend the first two to three weeks of the school year establishing structure in their classrooms (Doyle, 1979; Rink, 1993; Siedentop & Tannehill, 2000; Soar & Soar, 1979; Wynne & Ryan, 1997). Class routines and rules need to be internalized by your students and this takes time as your students practice and learn the class routines and rules.

TASK 1
Inventory of Behavior & Class Management Techniques
Interview/Self-Evaluation Format Worksheet

Student Teacher _____

Cooperating Teacher _____   **Date** _____
Or
Practicing Teacher _____   **Date** _____

<u>Behavior Management</u>

1.   Is there a school-wide or departmental disciplinary policy? If so, please describe it.

_____

_____

_____

2.   What is your (CT's or PT's) philosophy of behavior management?

_____

_____

_____

3.   How do you (CT or PT) encourage or reinforce appropriate student behavior. Describe rewards that you use?

_____

_____

_____

4.   What are some common behavior problems?   How can these be prevented?

_____

_____

_____

3

5. How do you (CT or PT) deal with inappropriate student behavior? What behavior management techniques do you use?

_____

_____

6. How would you (CT or PT) handle the following problems?

Not dressing for activity (if required): _____

Not participating: _____

Inappropriate language: _____

Acting out: _____

Fighting: _____

Carrying weapons: _____

Smoking: _____

Alcohol consumption: _____

Drug Use: _____

Explosive situations: _____

Talking back:_____

Other (describe): _____

7. What other management guidelines can you (CT or PT) suggest to help with effective behavior management?

_____

_____

Class Management

1. Describe the class routines you (CT or PT) use to establish good class structure.

Preparing the gymnasium _____

_____

Students entering class _____

_____

Dressing out _____

_____

Roll call _____

_____

Getting students' attention & giving directions _____

_____

Equipment distribution & collection _____

_____

Organizing groups or teams _____

_____

Fire drill _____

_____

Students leaving class _____

_____

Other routines _____

_____

2.   Describe your (CT or PT) class rules and consequences.

_____

_____

_____

_____

_____

_____

_____

_____

_____

Questionnaire adapted from:

Markos, N., & Boyce, B.A. (1999). What is your class management IQ? *Strategies,12*(6), 13-15.

Randall, L. (1992). *The student teacher's handbook for physical education.* Champaign, IL: Human Kinetics.

TASK 2
Attending to Inappropriate Behavior

The first few weeks of school are critical in terms of establishing class structure with your students (Doyle, 1979; Rink, 1993; Siedentop & Tannehill, 2000; Soar & Soar, 1979; Wynne & Ryan, 1997). It is during this initial time period that you will set the tone and expectations for the rest of the school year. Basically, you have two choices: (a) ignore inappropriate behavior, leading to an increase in student misbehavior until you lose all control of your class or (b) attend to and quickly correct student misbehavior, leading to a decrease in "student testing behaviors" (e.g., talking out of turn, reckless behavior in the gymnasium, failure to follow the teacher's instruction, etc.). Obviously, the ability to quickly recognize and correct off-task or inappropriate behavior of students is important because it will help you establish effective class structure with your students.

When teachers do not actively attend to student misbehavior, it may be due to several reasons: (a) a lack of confidence on the part of the teacher causing him/her to employ the "ignore it and maybe it will go away" philosophy or (b) a true lack of awareness related to the students' misbehavior, which may be a result of a teacher's focus on the lesson and not on the students that he/she is attempting to teach. Both of these reasons are typical scenarios for student teachers.

Once classroom structure has been established at the start of the school year, the teacher may elect to ignore some types of inappropriate behavior. Graham, Holt/Hale & Parker (2001) cited three situations where a teacher might choose to ignore student misbehavior: (a) if it is short in duration and not likely to spread, (b) if it is insignificant and/or (c) dealing with behavior would call undue attention to it.

Goal Setting Model for Dealing with this Problem/Issue

1. Identify the Problem – The **CT** (cooperating teacher) may note the **ST's** (student teacher) failure to deal effectively with students' inappropriate testing behaviors or to ignore misbehaving students. Some of the symptoms of this problem are: (a) persistent off-task behavior by students, (b) students take a long time to stop after a freeze signal is given and/or (c) students are inattentive during teacher's direction. In contrast, some of the ST's or teacher's symptoms are: (a) giving directions even though the ST/PT does not have the students' complete attention, (b) talking over the students' talking and/or (c) completely ignoring or being unaware of students who misbehave. The **PT** (practicing teacher) may also notice that students are not responding to his/her directions and some of the symptoms alluded to in the previous section may emerge in his/her class.

2. Collect Baseline Data – The **CT** can make a list of misbehaving students with elapsed time between when the misbehavior begins and when the **ST** starts to deal with the misbehaving student(s).

7

The **PT** will need to enlist the help of a peer teacher/partner (**P**) in order to collect information on this task. The **P** will make a list of misbehaving students with elapsed time between when the PT noted the misbehavior and when the PT starts to deal with the misbehaving student(s). Videotaping a class is another way to collect data on student behavior. However, the video camera must be set up to record the entire class in order to collect accurate information on all of the students.

Example:

Student's name	Elapsed time*
Ann	12 sec.
Joe	30 sec.
Chris	45 sec.
Terry	25 sec

Average number of seconds = 28 seconds (112 sec. divided by 4)
* Time between onset of inappropriate behavior and when action taken

---

3. Set Specific Goal(s) – Set a single long term goal (LTG) and/or a series of progressive short term goals (STGs) which will lead to the attainment of the long term goal.

For example, a LTG might be:

> *Deal with each student misbehavior within 3 seconds.*

Examples of STGs to achieve a LTG might be:

> *Deal with each student misbehavior within 20 seconds* (STG #1)
> *Deal with each student misbehavior within 10 seconds* (STG #2)
> *Deal with each student misbehavior within 5 seconds* (STG #3)
> *Deal with each student misbehavior within 3 seconds* (LTG)

Note: These goals treat all student misbehavior within the same time constraints, and sometimes accommodations need to be made for students with special needs. For example, a child with autism may require longer to stop and attend to the teacher after the freeze signal is given. Therefore, a second goal may need to be established for this student.

4. Outline Specific Strategies to Help ST Reach LTG (Suggested Strategies)

    a. 3-step strategy (steps 1 & 2 involve CT's/P's help) (information adapted from Boyce, 1997):

        1) Step 1 – The CT/P is positioned at the back of the class. When a student misbehaves, the CT/P walks in the general direction of that student, thus alerting the ST/PT. At that point, the ST/PT has 10 seconds (STG #2) to find and deal with the student.

        2) Step 2 – The CT/P is still positioned at the back of the class. This time when a student misbehaves, the CT/P simply raises his/her hand, thus alerting the ST. Again, the ST/PT has 5 seconds (STG #3) to locate and handle the situation.

        3) Step 3 – The ST/PT is on their own and must identify and handle the misbehavior situation.

    b. Other suggested strategies:

- Teach and practice class rules and routines; give feedback on student progress
- Use positive interactions with students before misbehavior occurs
- Don't treat students differently
- Use behavior prompting
- Teach students to be responsible for their own behavior (Hellison's [1995] Social Responsibility model)
- Constantly scan the class
- Keep all students in your line of sight at all times
- Use proximity praise for those students who are behaving
- Use physical proximity
- Use aggressive waiting
- Play games/activities that require listening and following directions
- Keep moving throughout the class
- Grouping – keep problem children apart
- Consistent consequences for misbehavior
- Deal with inappropriate behavior quickly
- Place "problem students" near the teacher
- Learn the students' names
- Use positive reinforcement

5. Collect data to check on the ST's/PT's progress throughout the week (at least 3-4x at the elementary level and 2-3x at the secondary level [block or portion of the block schedule])

```
Example:  Class #1

                Student's name              Elapsed time

                Ann                         10 sec.
                Joe                         20 sec.
                Chris                       16 sec.
                Terry                       14 sec

Compute average number of seconds of Class #1 = 15 seconds
```

Compare these data to your STGs and LTG:

```
Class #1 average seconds – 15 sec.
Attained STG #1 (20 sec.) but not STGs #2 (10 sec.) & #3 (5 sec.)
or LTG (3 sec.)
```

Repeat process for the other classes

6. Collect and compare post test data to your LTG

```
        Example:  Post test class

                Student's name              Elapsed time

                Sarah                       3 sec.
                John                        2 sec.
                Shawn                       4 sec.
                Traci                       3 sec

        POST TEST Data Average seconds – 3  sec.        Attained LTG
```

7. If you did not achieve the LTG – revise strategy and/or goal and continue to work toward the LTG with the revisions in place. Note: You can revise your strategies and/or STGs at any point during the process.

TASK 2
Attending to Inappropriate Behavior
Systematic Observation Worksheet

ST/PT _____   **School** _____
Date _____

Application of Goal Setting Model

Step 1 – Identify Problem – Not Attending to Inappropriate Student Behavior

Step 2 – Collect Baseline Data

> **CT/P** makes a list of misbehaving students with elapsed time between when the **CT/P** noted the misbehavior and when the **ST/PT** started to attend to the student's behavior.

Student's Name	Elapsed Time

Calculated Average Time per student _____

<u>Step 3</u> – Set Specific a LTG and/or Specific STGs – state these in observable terms
(e.g., time, percentage, number of students, etc).

LTG _____

STG #1_____

STG #2_____

STG #3_____

<u>Step 4</u> – List Strategies to Help You Attain Your LTG – See "Suggested Strategies"
under #4

1. _____
   _____
   _____
2. _____
   _____
3. _____
   _____
4. _____
   _____
5. _____
   _____

<u>Step 5</u> – Collect data throughout the week (3-4x elementary or 2-3x secondary level)

Class   #1   #2   #3   #4   (circle one)

Student's Name	Elapsed Time

Calculated Average Time per student _____

Compare Average Time to Your STGs & LTG:

Average Time _____

List Goal(s) You Achieved _____

_____

Make multiple copies of this page

Step 6 – Collect Post Test Data and Compare average to Your LTG

Post Test Class

Student's Name	Elapsed Time

Calculated Average Time per student _____

Compare Average Time to Your LTG:

Average Time _____   Achieved LTG—YES   or   NO (circle one)

Discuss your results: (for example: what strategies worked best, what goal
difficulties did you experience, or what did you learn)

_____

_____

_____

<u>Step 7</u> – If you did not achieve your LTG – Review Strategies and/or STGs and continue to work. Please note that you can modify strategies or STGs at any point in this process.

Space provided for ST/PT to review Strategies and review goals (if needed):

_____

_____

_____

_____

TASK 3
Lag Time

One of the most difficult routines to teach students is "stopping" their activity and "listening" to the teacher (Graham, Holt/Hale, & Parker, 2001). One indicator of the teacher's ability to get students' attention is referred to as "lag time." Lag time is defined as the seconds/minutes that elapse between the teacher's direction/request for students to stop and listen, and the last student who complies with that request. For example, a teacher may give a "freeze" signal and then wait for all students to comply; the time that passes between the signal and the last student to freeze is the "lag time."

Lag times may also have transition time built into them. For example, a teacher may direct students to get a piece of equipment and find a space to practice a given skill. In this case, the lag time would be inherently longer due to the built-in transition time.

The teacher's expectations of lag time may need to be adjusted based on the student population. For instances, a child with a hearing deficiency may need longer to comply with a teacher's verbal directions because this student may take their cues from other students in the class.

Goal Setting Model for Dealing with this Issue

1. Identify the Issue – Lag times that are longer than necessary

2. Collect Baseline Data – The **CT** (cooperating teacher) lists the lag time instances for various situations. It would also be helpful if the **CT** would give a one or two-word description of the activity the students are engaged in (e.g., freezing, equipment distribution, etc.). This information will let the **ST** (student teacher) know what activities (e.g., equipment distribution—time is exceptionally long, etc.) he/she needs to work on. If there is transition time involved in the lag time, a "t" can be placed by the listed time and activity.

    The **PT** (practicing teacher) can collect this information on their own by using a stopwatch to record their lag time incidences. The **PT** may not have time to record the activity students are engaged in just the lag times, but they should note if the lag time involves a transition "t." Additionally, the **PT** may enlist the help of a **P** (partner) or videotape lessons to collect information not only on elapsed time but also on the activity (freeze, changing stations, etc.) related to the lag time episode.

    > Example:
    >   1. 12 sec (freeze)
    >   2. 4 sec (freeze)
    >   3. 30 sec (equipment) – t
    >   4. 15 sec (behavior request)
    >   5. 35 sec (change stations) – t
    >   6. 5 sec (freeze)
    >   Calculate lag time w/out transition – <u>9 seconds</u> (36 divided by 4)
    >   Calculate lag time w/ transition - <u>16.8 seconds</u> (101 divided by 6)

16

3.   Set a Specific Goal(s) – Set a single long-term goal (LTG) and/or a series of progressive short-term goals (STGs) which will lead to the attainment of the long-term goal.

For example, a LTG goal might be:

> *Lag time of 2 seconds or less (without transitions)*
> *Lag time of 10 seconds or less (with transitions)*

Examples of STGs to achieve the LTG might be:

Lag time goals without transitions:

Lag time of 8 seconds or less	(STG #1)
Lag time of 5 seconds or less	(STG #2)
Lag time of 2 seconds or less	(LTG)

Lag times goals with transitions:

Lag time of 20 seconds or less	(STG #1)
Lag time of 15 seconds or less	(STG #2)
Lag time of 10 seconds or less	(LTG)

Note: These goals treat the lag time expectations for all students with the same time constraints. Sometimes accommodations need to be made for students with special needs. For example, a child with autism may require longer to stop and attend to the teacher after the freeze signal is given. Therefore, a second goal may need to be established for this student.

4.   Outline Specific Strategies to Help **ST** Reach LTG Goal (Suggested Strategies)

- Keep directions short and simple
- Check for understanding of directions (if needed)
- The freeze or attention signal must be loud enough for students to hear, or if the signal is visual it must be seen by all students
- Use aggressive waiting
- Play games/activities that require listening and following directions (see Graham, et al., 2001; for examples of these games)
- Teach students the routines related to equipment distribution, freezing, finding a good work/practice space (personal space), and practice these routines

- Early in school year strictly enforce rules with consequences
- Use hustles such as count downs

5.   Collect data to check on the **ST's/PT's** progress throughout the week (at least 3-4x at the elementary level and 2-3x at the secondary level [block or portion of the block schedule])

Example: Class #1

1. 5 (freeze)
2. 10 (behavior request)
3. 20 (find a personal space) – t
4. 12 (behavior request)
5. 8 (return equipment) –t
6. 5 (freeze)

Calculate lag time without transition – <u>8 seconds</u> (32 divided by 4)
Calculate lag time with transition—<u>10 seconds</u> (60 divided by 6)

Compare these data to your STGs and LTG:

Class #1

Average seconds without transition – 8 sec.	Attained STG #1 (8 sec. or less) but not STG #2 (5 sec. or less) or LTG (2 sec. or less)
Average seconds with transition – 10 sec.	Attained STG #1 & 2 (20&15 sec. or less) and LTG (10 sec. or less)

Repeat process for the other classes

6.   Collect and compare post test data to your LTG

Example: Post test class

        1.   1 sec. (freeze)
        2.   3 sec. (behavior request)
        3.   10 sec. (get equipment) – t
        4.   2 sec. (freeze)
        5.   8 sec. (change stations) – t
        6.   5 sec. (find a personal/work space) – t

Average seconds without transition – 2 sec.   Attained LTG (2 sec. or less)

Average seconds with transition – 4.8 sec.   Attained LTG (10sec. or less)

7.   If you did not achieve the LTG – revise strategy and/or goal and continue to work
       toward the LTG with the revisions in place. Note: You can revise your
       strategies and/or STGs at any point during the process.

TASK 3
Lag Time
Systematic Observation Worksheet

ST/PT _____   **School** _____

Date _____

<u>Application of Goal Setting Model</u>

<u>Step 1</u> – Identify Issue – Getting the Lag Time under Control

<u>Step 2</u> – Collect Baseline Data

      CT/PT can make a list of the elapsed time between when the **ST/PT** made a request and when the last student complied with that request. Also note the activity and if there is transition "t" involved. The **PT** may want to only record the elapsed times and transition "t."

Elapsed Time	Activity & Transition (if occurred) "t"

Calculate Average Time without transition   _____

Calculate Average Time with transition   _____

<u>Step 3</u> – Set Specific a LTG and/or Specific STGs – State these in observable terms
(e.g., time in seconds).

Without Transition:

LTG _____

STG #1_____

STG #2_____

With Transition:

LTG _____

STG #1 _____

STG #2 _____

<u>Step 4</u> - List Strategies to Help You attain your LTGs (with & without transition) – See
"Suggested Strategies" under #4.

1. _____
_____
_____
2. _____
_____
3. _____
_____
4. _____
_____
5. _____
_____

<u>Step 5</u> – Collect data throughout week (3-4x elementary or 2-3x secondary level)

Class   #1   #2   #3   #4   (circle one)

Elapsed Time	Activity & Transition (if occurred) "t"

Calculate your Average Lag Time without Transition: _____

Compare Average Time to Your STGs & LTG without Transition:

Average Time _____   List Goal(s) You Achieved _____

Calculate your Average Lag Time with Transition: _____

Compare Average Time to Your STGs & LTG with Transition:

Average Time _____   List Goal(s) You Achieved _____

Make multiple copies of this page

<u>Step 6</u> – Collect Post Test Data and Compare Average to Your LTG

Post Test Class

Elapsed Time	Activity & Transition (if occurred) "t"

Calculated the Average Lag Time without Transition _____

Compare Average Time to Your LTG:

Average Time _____   Achieved LTG – YES or NO (circle one)

Calculated the Average Lag Time with Transition _____

Compare Average Time to Your LTG:

Average Time _____   Achieved LTG – YES or NO (circle one)

Discuss your results: (for example: what strategies worked best, what goal difficulties did you encounter, or what did you learn)

_____

_____

_____

Step 7 – If you did not achieve your LTG – Review Strategies and/or STGs and continue to work. Please note that you can modify your strategies and/or STGs at any point during this process.

Space provided for **ST/PT** to review Strategies and review goals (if needed):

_____

_____

_____

_____

TASK 4
On-Task Behavior
Systematic Observation

The time a student spends practicing a given skill is critical in terms of the amount of time an individual needs to learn that skill. In order for teachers to help enhance the learning process, they must provide their students with many opportunities to practice both motor skills (sport, dance, outdoor education, fundamental motor patterns/skill themes, etc.) as well as physical fitness activities. However, the teacher's provision of practice opportunity does not always translate into the students' participation. Therefore, the students' ability to engage in practice opportunities cannot be assumed and teachers must teach their students to be on-task. Teachers can accomplish this by monitoring practice opportunities and correcting inappropriate or "off-task" behavior when it occurs.

Student "on-task behavior" is a good indicator of whether or not a teacher has established structure in the classroom. High "on-task behavior" (e.g., 95% of the students engaged in practicing a skill) is indicative of a teacher who has spent time teaching and reinforcing the importance of being on-task.

"On-task behavior" does not address student success, which is typically associated with Academic Learning Time - Physical Education (ALT-PE) (Siedentop, Tousignant & Parker, 1982). The measurement of student success will be covered later in this text. For now, we will focus on on-task behavior as it relates to the students' compliance to practicing skill(s) that the teacher designates.

Goal Setting Model for Dealing with this Issue

1.   Identify the Issue – Measuring students' on-task behavior

2.   Collect Baseline Data – The **CT/PT** (cooperating teacher/practicing teacher) records on-task behavior using a placheck (planned activity check) procedure (Siedentop, 1991).

Placheck involves the following:
a.   Scanning (usually left to right) and counting/recording the number of students who are <u>NOT</u> engaged in the designated task (e.g., practicing the tennis serve, listening to instructions, participating in a cardio-vascular workout)
b.   This scanning process usually takes about 10-15 seconds to complete
c.   Once a student is scanned and counted, the **CT/PT** cannot return to that student in that particular interval if his/her behavior changes
d.   This process should be completed every 2 minutes (scanning interval)

Calculating the percentage of students on-task, requires the following steps:

a.   Count the number of intervals scanned (e.g., in a 30 minute class the **CT/PT** would scan @ 15 times [once every 2 minutes])

b.   Count the total number of students in the class (e.g., 30 students)

c.   Multiply the total number of intervals (e.g., 15) by the number of students (e.g., 30) to get the total score (15 x 30 = 450)

d.   Count the total number of students who were off-task across the 15 intervals (e.g., 30 students were off-task)

e.   Subtract the number of off-task students from the total number (450-30 = 420)

f.   Calculate a ratio (420/450 = x /100) to get the percentage of on-task students. In this case x = 93.3% of the students are on-task.

Example:

Total number of intervals scanned = 15

Total number of students = 30

Multiply number of intervals by total number of students (15 x 30) =   450 (this number represents the total number of possible opportunities for on-task behavior)

Intervals recorded (off-task students):

I	NO	I	NO
1.	1	9.	3
2.	1	10.	5
3.	2	11.	3
4.	0	12.	1
5.	1	13.	5
6.	1	14.	2
7.	0	15.	5
8.	0		

Count off-task students across 15 intervals = 30 students
I = interval number & NO = number of off-task students

Subtract 30 from 450 (450-30) = 420 (gives total number of students who are on-task)

Calculate ratio $\frac{420}{450} = \frac{x}{100}$

x = 93.3% of the students are on-task

---

3. Set Specific Goals – Set a single long term goal (LTG) and/or a series of progressive short term goals (STG), which will lead to the attainment of the long term goal.

For example, a LTG goal might be:

> *95% of students are on-task*

Examples of STGs to achieve the LTG might be:

75% of students are on-task	(STG #1)
85% of students are on-task	(STG #2)
90% of students are on-task	(STG #3)
95% of students are on-task	(LTG)

Note: These goals treat all student off-task behavior with the same percentage specification(s); sometimes accommodations need to be made for students. For example, a student with ED (emotional disorder) may require a lower percentage of time for on-task behavior. Therefore, the **CT** and **ST/PT** might elect to count that students behavior separately and/or set a second set of goals to accommodate the needs of this student or the needs of other students with special needs.

4. Outline Specific Strategies to Help **ST/PT** Reach LTG Goal (Suggested Strategies)

- Practice, monitor and give feedback to students related to their on-task or off-task behavior
- Use aggressive waiting
- Use proximity praise to encourage on-task behavior
- Keep student wait time to a minimum, so you don't have students waiting in lines for their turn
- Begin your class promptly
- Keep the lesson pace moving; don't give them time to get off-task
- Use extensions and challenges to motivate students
- Clearly define rewards (e.g., equipment collectors – "PE helpers") for students who are on-task and consequences for off-task behavior (e.g., consult with parents)
- Whole class challenges – present an award to the class for the highest on-task behavior

- Modify on-task expectations for students with special needs by setting different/additional goals for these individuals
- If equipment is limited, use a peer teaching style so that only half of the students use the equipment at one time. The use of this teaching style would require the teacher to re-define "on-task" to include those students who were actively engaged in peer teaching responsibilities
- If equipment is limited, use a stations format with different equipment at each station

5. Collect data to check on the **ST/PT's** Progress—throughout the week (at least 3-4x at the elementary level and 2-3x at the secondary level [block or portion of the block schedule]).

Example: Class #1

Total number of intervals scanned = 35 (block class 1 hour and 10 minutes), the 35 intervals represents one scan per every 2 minutes

Total number of students = 40

Multiply number of intervals by total number of students (35 x 40) = 1,400 (on-task opportunities)

Intervals recorded (off-task students):

I	NO	I	NO	I	NO	I	NO
1.	6	10.	10	19.	5	28.	2
2.	6	11.	5	20.	5	29.	4
3.	7	12.	3	21.	3	30.	10
4.	5	13.	1	22.	7	31.	2
5.	4	14.	5	23.	8	32.	3
6.	3	15.	10	24.	7	33.	9
7.	5	16.	5	25.	5	34.	5
8.	10	17.	5	26.	5	35.	5
9.	5	18.	0	27.	5		

Count off-task students across the 35 intervals = 185 students
I = interval number & N = number of off-task students

Subtract 185 from 1400 (1400-185) = 1215 (gives total number of students who are on-task)

Calculate ratio $\frac{1215}{1400} = \frac{x}{100}$

x = 86.8% of the students are on-task

Compare these data to your STGs and LTG:

Class #1	
87% of students were on-task	Achieved STG #1 (75% on-task) & STG #2 (85% on-task) but not STG #3 (90 % on-task) or LTG (95% on-task)

Repeat this process for the other classes

6.   Collect and compare post test data to your LTG

Example: Post test class

Total number of intervals scanned = 35 (block class 1 hour and 10 minutes)

Total number of students = 40

Multiply number of intervals by total number of students (35 x 40) = 1,400 students on-task

Intervals recorded (off-task students):

I	NO	I	NO	I	NO	I	NO
1.	1	10.	3	19.	5	28.	2
2.	1	11.	5	20.	5	29.	4
3.	2	12.	3	21.	0	30.	5
4.	5	13.	1	22.	7	31.	2
5.	4	14.	5	23.	1	32.	5
6.	3	15.	2	24.	7	33.	3
7.	3	16.	2	25.	5	34.	1
8.	1	17.	2	26.	1	35.	0
9.	0	18.	0	27.	0		

Count off-task students across 35 intervals = 100 students
I = interval & NO = number

Subtract 100 from 1400 (1400-100) = 1300 (gives total no. of students who are on-task)

Calculate ratio $\frac{1300}{1400} = \frac{x}{100}$

x = 93% of the students are on-task

Compare these data to your LTG:

Post test	
93% of students were on-task	Did Not Achieved LTG (95% on-task)

7.   If you did not achieve the LTG – revise strategy and/or STG goal(s) and continue to work toward the LTG with the revisions in place. <u>Note:</u> You can revise your strategies and/or STGs at any point during the process.

TASK 4
On-Task Behavior
Systematic Observation Worksheet

ST/PT _____   **School** _____
Date _____

Application of Goal Setting Model

Step 1 – Identify Issue – Getting My Students On-task

Step 2 – Collect Baseline Data – The **CT/PT** records on-task behavior using a placheck (planned activity check) procedure.

Placheck involves the following:

a.   Scanning (usually left to right) and counting/recording the number of students who are <u>NOT</u> engaged in the designated task (e.g., practicing the tennis serve, listening to instructions, participating in a cardio-vascular workout)

b.   This scan usually takes about 10-15 seconds to complete

c.   Once a student is scanned and counted the **CT/PT** cannot return to that student if his/her behavior changes

d.   This process can be completed every 2 minutes (scanning interval)

Calculating the percentage of students on-task, requires the following steps:

a.   Count the number of intervals scanned (e.g., in a 30 minute class the **CT/PT** would scan @ 15 times [once, every 2 minutes])

b.   Count the total number of students in the class (e.g., 30 students)

c.   Multiply the total number of intervals (e.g., 15) by the number of students (e.g., 30) to get the total score (15 x 30 = 450)

d.   Count the total number of students who were off-task across the 15 intervals (e.g., 30 students were off-task)

e.   Subtract the number of off-task students from the total number (450-30 = 420)

f.   Calculate a ratio (420/450 = x /100) to get the percentage of on-task students, in this case x = 93.3% of the students who are on-task

31

Baseline Data

Interval Number	No. of St. off-task	Interval Number	No. of St. off-task
1.		19.	
2		20.	
3.		21.	
4.		22.	
5.		23.	
6.		24.	
7.		25.	
8.		26.	
9.		27.	
10.		28.	
11.		29.	
12.		30.	
13.		31.	
14.		32.	
15.		33.	
16.		34.	
17.		35.	
18.		36.	

Calculate On-Task Percentage _____

Use the steps a. through f. provided on the previous page to help you make this calculation

Step 3 – Set Specific a LTG and/or Specific STGs – state these in observable terms (e.g., percentage of students who are on-task).

Goals Related to On-Task Behavior of Students:

LTG _____

STG #1_____

STG #2_____

STG #3 _____

Set separate goal for students with special needs (if necessary):

LTG _____

Step 4 – List Strategies to Help You attain your LTGs (high on-task percentages) – See "Suggested Strategies" under #4.

1. _____
   _____

2. _____
   _____

3. _____
   _____

4. _____
   _____

5. _____
   _____

<u>Step 5</u> – Collect data throughout week (3-4x elementary or 2-3x secondary level)

Class   #1   #2   #3   #4   (circle one)

Interval Number	No. of St. off-task	Interval Number	No. of St. off-task
1.		19.	
2		20.	
3.		21.	
4.		22.	
5.		23.	
6.		24.	
7.		25.	
8.		26.	
9.		27.	
10.		28.	
11.		29.	
12.		30.	
13.		31.	
14.		32.	
15.		33.	
16.		34.	
17.		35.	
18.		36.	

Calculate On-Task Percentage _____

Compare Calculated Percentage to Your STGs & LTG for On-Task Behavior:

Percentage _____   List Goal(s) You Achieved _____

Make multiple copies of this page

Step 6 – Collect Post Test Data and Compare Calculated Percentage to Your LTG

Post Test Class

Interval Number	No. of St. off-task	Interval Number	No. of St. off-task
1.		19.	
2		20.	
3.		21.	
4.		22.	
5.		23.	
6.		24.	
7.		25.	
8.		26.	
9.		27.	
10.		28.	
11.		29.	
12.		30.	
13.		31.	
14.		32.	
15.		33.	
16.		34.	
17.		35.	
18.		36.	

Calculate On-Task percentage _____

Compare Calculated Percentage to Your LTG:

　　　　Percentage _____　　Achieved LTG – YES　or　NO　(circle one)

Discuss your results: (for example: what strategies worked best, what goal difficulties did you encounter, or what did you learn)

_____

_____

_____

<u>Step 7</u> – If you did not achieve your LTG – Review Strategies and/or STGs and continue to work. Please note that you modify your strategies and/or STGs at any point during the process.

Space provided for **ST/PT** to review strategies and review goals (if needed):

_____

_____

_____

_____

TASK 5
Keeping Your Back to the Wall

The ability to keep your students in your line of sight at all times is crucial not only from a class/behavioral management perspective but also from a safety standpoint. In fact, a large number of lawsuits (some sources report over 50 percent of all lawsuits in physical education and sport) stem from a lack of supervision (Berryhill & Jarman, 1979; Merriman, 1993). One way to view your entire class is to position yourself so that you can see all of your students. This observation technique is referred to as "*Back to the Wall.*" The back to the wall (BTW) observation technique is especially helpful when establishing a structured learning environment in the first 2-3 weeks of school when constant monitoring is necessary as well as when classes are behaviorally challenging or difficult to manage. Teachers should be mindful of their positioning at all times standing in the middle of a class may hinder a teacher's ability to view all students. It is possible to give skill related feedback to one student while keeping the other students in your line of sight but it does require an awareness of your location. The BTW technique is also useful in an outdoor setting. However, since a "wall" is not present, the teacher should simply keep students in his/her line of sight at all times.

It is interesting to note that even experienced teachers are not always aware of the back to the wall positioning technique (Graham et al., 2001). For beginning as well as veteran teachers, this BTW technique is important to ensure the students' safety as well as assist with behavior/class management issues.

<u>Goal Setting Model for Dealing with this Issue</u>

1. Identify the Issue – At times the **CT/P** (cooperating teacher / partner) may observe the **ST/PT's** (student teacher/practicing teacher) failure to keep students in their line of sight.

2. Collect Baseline Data – Ask the **CT/P** to count the number of times that the **ST/PT** does not keep their back to the wall (BTW). It would also be helpful if the **CT/P** recorded the student(s)' names who the **ST/PT** cannot see. Sometimes students deliberately position themselves outside the teacher's viewing area. Also, knowing the situation when the BTW principle was violated may be useful to the **ST/PT**. For example, perhaps the **ST/PT** fails to keep his/her BTW when giving directions.

Example:		
<u>BTW occurrences</u>	<u>Student(s) name</u>	<u>Situation</u>
I	Ann/Jerrry	roll call
I	Bill	giving directions
I	Cathy	student practice
I	Sam	student practice
Number of BTW occurrences in this class = 4		

3.   Set Specific Goals – Set a single long term goal (LTG) and/or a series of progressive short term goals (STG) which will lead to the attainment of the long term goal.

For example, a LTG might be:

> *No more than one BTW occurrence per class.*

Examples of STGs to achieve a LTG might be to:

Only 6 BTW occurrences per class.	(STG #1)
Only 4 BTW occurrences per class.	(STG #2)
Only 2 BTW occurrences per class.	(STG #3)
No more than one BTW occurrence per class.	(LTG)

4.   Outline Specific Strategies to Help ST/PT Reach LTG (Suggested Strategies)

- Constantly scan the class
- Keep all students in your line of sight at all times
- Position yourself on the outside of the class
- Use a half circle organizational pattern when giving skill demonstrations
- Bring students to you, to give correctional feedback
- Keep moving throughout the class
- Note the students who are frequently out of your line of sight and attend to these individuals (maybe they are out of your line of sight for a reason – misbehavior)
- Note the situations when you fail to keep your BTW and attend to these
- Monitor student activities from perimeter of the class
- Organize equipment & boundaries so that it is very difficult for students to be out of your line of sight
- When giving information or feedback, position yourself so that the class and all individuals are in front of you
- When dealing with off-task students, make sure you can see the rest of the class
- In lesson plans, organize class and activities to assure that you keep your BTW

5. Collect data to check on the **ST/PT's** Progress throughout the week (at least 3-4x at the elementary level and 2x at the secondary level [block or portion of the block schedule])

Example: Class #1

BTW occurrences	Student(s) name	Situation
I	Susie/John	skill demo
I	Chris	giving directions
I	John	student practice
I	Pat	student practice
I	Michelle/Mike	student practice
I	Shelia/John	student practice

Number of BTW occurrences per class = 6

Compare these data to your STGs and LTG:

Class #1 BTW occurrences = 6   Attained STG #1 (6 BTWs) but Not STG #2 (4 BTWs) & #3 (2 BTWs) or LTG (1 BTW)

Repeat process for the other classes

6. Collect and compare post test data to your LTG

Example: Post test class

BTW occurrences	Student(s) name	Situation
I	Susie/John	skill demo

Number of BTW occurrences per class = 1

Post Test Data = 1 BTW occurrence Attainted LTG

---

7.   If you did not achieve your long term goal (LTG), revise your strategy and/or goal and continue to work toward the LTG with the revisions in place.   Note: you can revise your strategies and/or STGs at any point during the process.

TASK 5
Keeping Your Back to the Wall
Systematic Observation Worksheet

ST/PT _____   **School** _____
Date _____

<u>Application of Goal Setting Model</u>

<u>Step 1</u> – Identify Problem – Keeping Your Back to the Wall (BTW)

<u>Step 2</u> – Collect Baseline Data

The **CT/P** should complete the following tasks:
1. Count the number of BTW occurrences
2. Record student(s)' names who the **ST/PT** cannot see
3. Note the situation when the BTW occurred

BTW occurrences	Student name(s)	Situation

Number of BTW occurrences at Baseline _____

Note students who are frequently out of the line of sight: _____

Note recurring situations: _____

41

Step 3 – Set Specific a LTG and/or Specific STGs – state these in observable terms
(e.g., number of BTW occurrences).

LTG _____

STG #1_____

STG #2_____

STG #3_____

Step 4 – List Strategies to Help You Attain Your LTG – See "Suggested Strategies"
under #4

1. _____
   _____
2. _____
   _____
3. _____
   _____
4. _____
   _____
5. _____
   _____

Step 5 – Collect data throughout week (3-4x elementary or 2-3x secondary level)

Class   #1   #2   #3   #4   (circle one)

BTW occurrences	Student name(s)	Situation

Number of BTW occurrences at Baseline _____

Note students who are frequently out of the line of sight: _____

Note recurring situations: _____

Compare BTW occurrences to Your STGs & LTG:

   BTW per Class _____   List Goal(s) You Achieved _____

                                   _____

Make multiple copies of this page

<u>Step 6</u> – Collect Post Test Data and Compare Average to Your LTG

Post Test Class

BTW occurrences	Student name(s)	Situation

Number of BTW occurrences at Baseline _____

Note students who are frequently out of the line of sight: _____

Note recurring situations: _____

Compare BTW occurrences to Your LTG:

BTW occurrence _____   Achieved LTG – YES or NO (circle one)

Discuss your results: (for example: what strategies worked best or goal difficulty or what did you learn)

_____

_____

_____

<u>Step 7</u> – If you did not achieve your LTG – Review Strategies and/or STGs and continue to work. Please note that you can modify strategies or STGs at any point in this process.

Space provided for **ST/PT** to review Strategies and review goals (if needed):

_____

_____

_____

_____

TASK 6
Positive and Corrective Interactions: How's Your Classroom Environment?

The amount of positive and corrective **behavior-related** feedback students receive is a measure of a classroom's emotional environment. If students hear only **behavior-related** corrective statements then the environment tends to be less positive. In contrast, if the environment is balanced with students receiving corrective behavior-related feedback when needed and positive feedback as an integral part of the classroom interaction then learning is supported. This balanced approach can facilitate appropriate student behavior as well as create an environment where students willingly attempt to learn skills and readily participate in fitness activities. A note of caution, teachers should avoid over-using positive feedback when it is not merited because this can lead to a devaluing of this type of feedback (e.g., praise) when the students actually deserve it (Brophy, 1982). *Also note that corrective statements related to skill patterns or fitness activities (e.g., keep your back flat against the bench when performing that lift or extend your arm in the direction of the throw) are not counted since these do not relate to behavioral corrections.*

Feedback can be delivered in both verbal and nonverbal ways. Teacher's smiles and approving head nods are examples of nonverbal positive interactions whereas frowns and scowls are indicative of nonverbal corrective/negative interactions. Verbal statements such as "good freeze" or "that's great" are examples of positive interactions and statements such as "Susie, I need everyone's attention, before I can start" or "John, please do what I asked you to do" are corrective in nature. Notice that negative or punitive statements are not classified as corrective behavior-related statements. This type of statement (e.g., "Ann that is the poorest excuse for standing in line quietly that I have ever seen" or "Bill, when will you ever learn to follow directions") will negatively impact the learning environment and may cause students to avoid participating in physical activities because they are afraid of being ridiculed (Brophy, 1982; Rink, 1996). Neutral interactions (e.g., teacher statement – "well that's interesting") can also occur as a part of the classroom exchange process, and does not seem to detract from to a positive classroom environment (Brophy & Good, 1986).

Another way to encourage a positive classroom environment is the use of students' names. By memorizing and using the students' first names the teacher demonstrates interest in each student and this can positively affect both classroom environment as well as a student's level of motivation (Harrison, Blakemore & Buck, 2001).

Goal Setting Model for Dealing with this Issue

1. Identify the Issue – Gauging the Classroom Environment – is it negative or positive? Is my name use equally distributed?

2. Collect Baseline Data – the **ST/PT** (student teacher/practicing teacher) can either use video recording camera with microphone or an audio recording devise to count the number and type of **behavior-related interactions** (positive, corrective or neutral) during a class, or the **CT** (cooperating teacher) can record this

information. It would also be helpful if the **ST/CT** or the **PT** noted the student(s)' gender or group interactions to see if there are any trends that might help the **ST/PT** better monitor their own interactions. For example, maybe males are only receiving corrective behavior-related feedback and females are getting only a few positive statements with the bulk of the positive statements made to the entire group. Please note that the use of the audio recording device will not capture the nonverbal interactions since they are not easily discernable with this type of media.

The **ST/CT** or **PT** will also need to note the number of females and males in their respective classes since this information will be important when interpreting the equity of responses related to the ratio of male to female interactions. For example, if there are equal numbers of females to males then a 1 to 1 ratio is appropriate but if there are twice as many females to males in the class then a 2 to 1 ratio of interactions is more equitable based on the number of female and male students in the actual class.

Example:

	Female	Male	Group
Positive	1111	11	11111111
Corrective (Behavior)	11	1111111111	111
Neutral	11111111	11111111	1111111
Name Use	111111111111	111111111111111	
Negative (sarcasm)	0	0	0

Totals: Positive: Female = 4 / Male = 2 / Group = 8 -> Combined = 14
　　　　Corrective: Female = 2 / Male = 11 / Group = 3 -> Combined = 16
　　　　Neutral:　 Female = 8 / Male = 8 / Group = 7 -> Combined = 23

　　　　Interpretation -> more corrective than positive 16 to 14
　　　　　　Ratio >1:1 (Corrective To Positive)

　　　　Name Use:　 Female = 12 / Male = 15

　　　　Interpretation -> more name used for males 15 to 12 (assumes an equal number of Ms to Fs)
　　　　　　Ratio >1:1 (males to females)

　　　　Negative = none observed across class (Great!!)

3.   Set a Specific Goal(s) – set a single long term goal (LTG) and/or a series of progressive short term goals (STG) which will lead to the attainment of the long term goal.

For example, a LTG might be:

Positive to Corrective:	*2 positives to every 1 corrective (secondary)*
	3 positives to every 1 corrective (elementary)
Name Use:	*Equal use of males to females (1 to 1 ratio)*
	Assuming an equal number of males to females
Negative:	*O negative comments*

Examples of STGs to achieve a LTG might be to:

Positive to Corrective:	*<1 positive to every 1 corrective (sec.)*	STG #1
	1 positive to every 1 corrective (sec.)	STG #2
	2 positives to every 1 corrective (sec.)	LTG
	1 positive to every 1 corrective (elem.)	STG #1
	2 positive to every 1 corrective (elem.)	STG #2
	3 positives to every 1 corrective (elem.)	LTG
Name Use:	*Not equal name use (3 to 1)*	STG #1
	Not equal name use (2 to 1)	STG #2
	Equal use of males to females (1 to 1)	LTG
	(Assumes equal numbers of Ms & Fs)	
Negative:	*4 negative comments*	STG #1
	2 negative comments	STG #2
	O negative comments	LTG

4.   Outline Specific Strategies to Help **ST/PT** Reach LTG (Suggested Strategies)

- Catch students doing good things and comment on them
- Memorize and use names as quickly as possible
- Position yourself on the outside of the class so you can see and comment
- Eliminate the negative in our thoughts
- Bring students to you to give correctional feedback. It is usually best not to confront a student in the presence of his/her peers.

- Pinpoint good behavior of students
- Make an effort to say something positive to every student in every class
- Establish a relationship with students and talk to them outside of class (e.g., at lunch, in the hallways, etc.)

5. Collect data to check on the **ST/PT's** progress throughout the week (at least 3-4x at the elementary level and 2x at the secondary level [block or portion of the block schedule])

Example: Class #1 (elementary level)

	Female	Male	Group
Positive	1111111111	111111111111	11111111
Corrective (Behavior)	11111	11111	11111
Neutral	11111111	1111111	11111
Name Use	11111111111	111111111111111	
Negative (sarcasm)	11	1	0

Totals: Positive: Female = 10 / Male = 12 / Group = 8 -> Combined = 30
        Corrective: Female = 5 / Male = 5 / Group = 5 -> Combined = 15
        Neutral: Female = 8 / Male = 7 / Group = 5 -> Combined = 20

Interpretation -> more positives than corrective – 30 to 15 (2 to 1 ratio)

Name Use: Female = 12 / Male = 15

Interpretation -> more name use for males 15 to 12   (>1 to 1 – M to F)
                 (assuming equal no. of males & females)

Negative = Female = 2 / Male = 1 -> Combined 3

Compare these data to your STGs and LTG:

Class #1 (elementary level)	
Positive to Corrective: 30 to 15	Attained STG #1 (< pos. to 1 corr.) & #2 (2 pos. to 1 corr.) not LTG (3 pos. to 1 corr.)
Name use: 12 to 15	Attained STG #1 (3 to 1) & #2 (2 to 1) not LTG (1 to 1)
Negative comments: 3	Attained STG #1 (4 neg.) not STG #2 (2 neg.) or LTG (0 neg.)

Repeat process for the other classes

6. Collect and compare post test data to your LTG

Example: Post test class

	Female	Male	Group
Positive	11111111111	111111111111111	11111111
Corrective (Behavior)	11111	11111	
Neutral	11111	11111	11111
Name Use	1111111111111	111111111111	
Negative (sarcasm)	0	0	0

Totals: Positive: Female = 12 / Male = 15 / Group = 8 -> Combined = 35
        Corrective: Female = 5 / Male = 5 / Group = 0 -> Combined = 10
        Neutral: Female = 5 / Male = 5 / Group = 5 -> Combined = 15

Interpretation -> more positive than corrective (35 to 10) (<3 to 1 ratio)
Attained LTG

Name Use: Female = 13 Male = 13

Interpretation -> name use equal 13 to 13 (equal no. of M & F) ratio 1 to 1
Attained LTG

Negative = none observed across class (Great!!) Attained LTG

7. If you did not achieve the LTG – revise strategy and/or goal and continue to work towards the LTG with the revisions in place. Note: You can revise your strategies and/or STGs at any point during the process.

TASK 6
Positive and Corrective Interactions: How's Your Classroom Environment?
Systematic Observation Worksheet

ST/PT _____   School _____
Date _____

Application of Goal Setting Model

Step 1 – Identify Problem – Gauging the Classroom Environment – Is it negative or positive related to **behavior-related feedback**? Is my name use equally distributed? Am I negative with the students?

Step 2 – Collect Baseline Data

The **PT and ST** (use of tape recorder) or **CT** (live observation) should complete the following tasks:

1.   Count the number of interaction occurrences
2.   Record this count under the correct category (female, male or group)
3.   Total and interpret the data

	Females	Males	Group
Positive			
Corrective (Behavior)			
Neutral			
Name Use			
Negative (sarcasm)			

Totals: Positive: Female = ____ / Male = ____ / Group = ____ -> Combined = ____
          Corrective: Female = ____ / Male = ____ / Group = ____ -> Combined = ____

Neutral:　　　Female = ____ / Male = ____ / Group = ____ -> Combined = ____

Interpret – Positives to Correctives (____ to ____) (calculate ratio) _____

Name Use:　　Female = ____ / Male = ____

Interpret – no. of name use (____ to ____) (calculate ratio) _____
(assumes equal females & males)

Negative:　　Female = ____ / Male = ____ / Group = ____ -> Combined = ____

Note: The **ST/CT** or **PT** will also need to note the number of females and males in their respective classes since this information will be important when interpreting the equity of responses related to the ratio of male to female interactions. For example, if there are equal numbers of females to males then a 1 to 1 ratio is appropriate but if there are twice as many females to males in the class then a 2 to 1 ratio of interactions is more equitable based on the number of female and male students in the actual class.

Step 3 – Set Specific a LTG and/or Specific STGs – state these in observable terms (e.g., number of interaction and/or name use occurrences).

Positive to Corrective interactions:

　　　LTG _____

　　　STG #1_____

　　　STG #2_____

Name Use:

　　　LTG _____

　　　STG #1_____

　　　STG #2_____

Negative interactions:

　　　LTG _____

　　　STG #1_____

　　　STG #2_____

Step 4 – List Strategies to Help You Attain your LTG – See "Suggested Strategies" under
#4

1. _____
_____
_____

2. _____
_____

3. _____
_____

4. _____
_____

5. _____
_____
_____

<u>Step 5</u> – Collect data throughout week (3-4x elementary or 2-3x secondary level)

Class   #1   #2   #3   #4   (circle one)

	Females	Males	Group
Positive			
Corrective (Behavior)			
Neutral			
Name Use			
Negative (sarcasm)			

Totals: Positive: Female = ____ / Male = ____ / Group = ____ -> Combined = ____
          Corrective: Female = ____ / Male = ____ / Group = ____ -> Combined = ____
          Neutral: Female = ____ / Male = ____ / Group = ____ -> Combined = ____

          Interpret – Postives to Correctives (_____ to _____) Calculate ratio _____
          List Goals Achieved: _____

          Name Use: Female = ____ / Male = ____

          Interpret – no. of name use (_____ to _____) Calculate Ratio _____
          (assumes equal females & males)
          List Goals Achieved: _____

          Negative: Female = ____ / Male = ____ / Group = ____ -> Combined = ____
          List Goals Achieved: _____

Make multiple copies of this page

Step 6 – Collect Post Test Data and Compare Average to Your LTG

Post Test Class

	Females	Males	Group
Positive			
Corrective (Behavior)			
Neutral			
Name Use			
Negative (sarcasm)			

Totals: Positive: Female = ____ / Male = ____ / Group = ____ -> Combined = ____
Corrective: Female = ____ / Male = ____ / Group = ____ -> Combined = ____
Neutral: Female = ____ / Male = ____ / Group = ____ -> Combined = ____

Interpret – Postives to Correctives (_____ to _____) Calculate ratio _____
Did Attain the LTG? YES or NO (circle one)

Name Use: Female = ____ / Male = ____

Interpret – no. of name use (_____ to _____) Calculate ratio _____
(assumes equal females & males)
Did Attain the LTG? YES or NO (circle one)

Negative: Female = ____ / Male = ____ / Group = ____ -> Combined = ____

Did Attain the LTG? YES or NO (circle one)

56

Discuss your results: (for example: what strategies worked best, what goal difficulties did you encounter, or what did you learn)

_____

_____

_____

Step 7 – If you did not achieve your LTG – Review Strategies and/or STGs and continue to work. Please note that you can modify strategies or STGs at any point in this process.

Space provided for **ST/PT** to review Strategies and review goals (if needed):

_____

_____

_____

_____

TASK 7
Time Spent on Class Management

In order to increase the amount of time a student spends practicing a sport or fitness-related skill, teachers must plan and implement lessons that minimize time spent on management tasks. Effective teachers must be good managers, since poor management practices result in lost practice time (Rink, 1996). Management tasks include a variety of responsibilities (e.g., taking class attendance, getting students into groups, distributing and collecting equipment, transitioning, providing directions for management activities, etc.). The key to minimizing managerial tasks is planning. Teachers must decide how students will be grouped and/or how equipment will be distributed prior to the students entering the gymnasium. For example, a teacher may post the names of teams and team members (e.g., arranging students into groups) for the day on a bulletin broad, thus saving valuable class time. Management time can also be optimized by using pre-established routines (e.g., use of signals for getting attention, transitioning, finding a partner, distributing equipment, etc.). **Management time also includes giving directions for management activities**. For example, a teacher might say, "When I say go, I need all students with birthdays in January and February to get a jump roll and find a personal space. Ready, go." Lastly, at middle and high school levels changing clothes for participation is a part of the management equation and this task also detracts from student fitness or skill development.

Goal Setting Model for Dealing with this Issue

1.   Identify the Issue – measuring the time spent on management tasks

2.   Collect Baseline Data – The **CT/P** (cooperating teacher/partner) lists management tasks and then records the time the **ST/PT** (student teacher/practicing teacher) spent on each task. In addition, a videotaped class can also be used to record management tasks and elapsed time spent on each task.

Calculate the percentage of time spent on managing class activities:
a.   List the management tasks and record the time spent on each task
b.   Sum the total amount of time in management
c.   Convert total management time into seconds (e.g., 1:30 seconds equals 90 seconds)
d.   Convert the total amount of time in class into seconds (30 minute class equals 1800 seconds or 60 minute class equals 3600 seconds)
e.   Compute a percentage ($90/1800 = x/100$) to get the percentage management time, in this case $x = 5\%$

Example:

List the management task and the corresponding time

roll call	2:30 minutes/seconds or 150 seconds
get attention	5 seconds
directions for finding a partner	10 seconds
transition (finding a partner)	<u>30 seconds</u>

Sum the total amount of management time

total time   3:15 min./sec.

Convert management time into seconds

3:15 equals $180 + 15 = 195$ seconds

Convert total class time into seconds

30 minute class equals 1800 seconds

Compute percentage

$195/1800 = x/100$
$x = 10.8\%$ of time spent on management tasks

3.   Set a Specific Goal(s) – set a single long term goal (LTG) and/or a series of progressive short term goals (STG) which will lead to the attainment of the long term goal.

For example, a LTG goal might be:

> *≤20% of time spent on management tasks*
> ***SUGGESTED Beginning Teacher Performance Standard (BTPS)****

<u>*Note:*</u> *(*)The "SUGGESTED Beginning Teacher Performance Standard (BTPS)" has been taken from the literature on teacher effectiveness and these standards are strongly suggested for use and appear in BOLD type. While these standards are for the most part achievable, sometimes this standard will need to be adjusted to meet the needs (low SES level of school, large class sizes, etc.) of your teaching situation.*

Examples of STGs to achieve the LTG might be:

> $\leq 30\%$ *of time spent on management tasks*   (STG #1)
> $\leq 25\%$ *of time spent on management tasks*   (STG #2)
> $\leq 20\%$ *of time spent on management tasks*   (LTG)

4.

- Practice routines related to managerial tasks (e.g., getting students' attention, transitions, etc.)
- Prepare equipment in advance (before class starts)
- Know how you will group your students in advance
- If you are using teams – post teams so students know ahead of time
- Use few transitions
- Post the day's activities for students to read prior to class
- Complete roll call as students are doing warm-up exercises
- Use hustles
- Give clear directions (bullet instructions) with prompts "When I say go"
- Use consistent format (e.g., whistle, stop collect equipment, rotate. etc.)
- Use multiple stations for equipment distribution
- Practice freeze games and set goals for students to achieve
- Be firm with students when establishing management routines
- Use the color or type of equipment to organize students into groups or activities
- Mark the gymnasium floor with "polyspots" or tape to help elementary school children quickly find a good personal space

5. Collect data to check on the **ST/PT's** progress throughout the week (at least 3-4x at the elementary level and 2-3x at the secondary level [block or portion of the block schedule])

Example: Class #1

List the management task and the corresponding time

roll call	2 minutes
get attention	15 seconds
give man. directions	1 minute
equipment dist.	1 minute
transition	30 seconds
switch stations	15 seconds
get attention	15 seconds
switch stations	15 seconds
transition	15 seconds
collect equipment	1 minute

Sum the total amount of management time

total time   6:45 min./sec.

Convert management time into seconds

6:45 equals   360 + 45 = 405 seconds

Convert total class time into seconds

30 minute class equals 1800 seconds

Compute percentage

405/1800 = x/100
x = 22.5% of time spent on management tasks

Compare these data to your STGs and LTG:

Class #1

22.5% time on management tasks   Achieved STG #1 ($\leq$30%) & STG #2 ($\leq$25%)
                                    but not LTG ($\leq$20%)

Repeat this process for the other classes

6.   Collect and compare post test data to your LTG

Example: Post test class

List the management task and the corresponding time

roll call	1:30 minutes
get attention	15 seconds
give man. directions	1 minute
equipment dist.	1 minute
transition	15 seconds
switch stations	15 seconds
get attention	15 seconds
switch stations	15 seconds
transition	15 seconds
collect equipment	45 minute

Sum the total amount of management time

total time   5:45 min./sec.

Convert management time into seconds

5:45 equals   300 + 45 = 345 seconds

Convert total class time into seconds

30 minute class equals 1800 seconds

Compute percentage

345/1800 = x/100
x = 19.2% of time spent on management tasks

Compare these data to your LTG:

```
Post test

19.2% spent on management          Achieved LTG (≤20%)

            ACHIEVED SUGGESTED BTPS (≤20%)
```

7.   If you did not achieve the LTG – revise strategy and/or STG goal(s) and continue to work towards the LTG with the revisions in place. Note: You can revise your strategies and/or STGs at any point during the process.

TASK 7
Time Spent on Class Management
Systematic Observation Worksheet

ST/PT _____   **School** _____
Date _____

Application of Goal Setting Model

Step 1 – Identify Issue – how much time do I spend on management tasks?

Step 2 – Collect Baseline Data –The **CT/P** lists management tasks and then records the time the **ST/PT** spent on each task.

Calculating the percentage of time spent managing requires the following steps:
a.   List the management tasks and record the time spent on each task
b.   Sum the total amount of time in management
c.   Convert total management time into seconds (e.g., 1:30 seconds equals 90 seconds)
d.   Convert the total amount of time in class into seconds (30 minute class equals 1800 seconds or 60 minute class equals 3600 seconds)
e.   Compute a percentage ($90/1800 = x/100$) to get the percentage management time, in this case $x = 5\%$

Baseline Data

Management Task	Time Spent on Management Task
1.	
2.	
3.	
4.	
5.	
6.	
7.	
8.	
9.	
10.	
11.	
12.	
13.	
14.	
15.	

Total Time _____

Calculate Time Spent on Management Tasks _____

Use the steps a. through e. provided on the previous page to help you make this calculation

Step 3 – Set Specific a LTG and/ or Specific STGs – state these in observable terms (e.g., percentage of total time spent on management tasks).

    Note: The LTG SHOULD reflect the Suggested BTPS of 20% or less.

Goals related to Time Spent on Management:

    LTG _____

    STG #1_____

    STG #2_____

    STG #3 _____

Step 4 - List Strategies to Help You Attain your LTGs (low management time) – See "Suggested Strategies" under #4.

    1. _____

    2. _____

    3. _____

    4. _____

    5. _____

Step 5 – Collect data throughout week (3-4x elementary or 2-3x secondary level)

Class   #1   #2   #3   #4   (circle one)

Management Task	Time Spent on Management Task
1.	
2.	
3.	
4.	
5.	
6.	
7.	
8.	
9.	
10	
11.	
12.	
13.	
14.	
15.	

Total Time _____

Calculate Percentage of Management Time _____

Compare Calculated Percentage to Your STGs & LTG:

Percentage _____   List Goal(s) You Achieved _____

Make multiple copies of this page

<u>Step 6</u> – Collect Post Test Data and Compare Calculated Percentage to Your LTG

Post Test Class

Management Task	Time Spent on Management Task
1.	
2.	
3.	
4.	
5.	
6.	
7.	
8.	
9.	
10	
11.	
12.	
13.	
14.	
15.	

Total Time _____

Calculate Percentage of Management Time _____

Compare Calculated Percentage to Your LTG:

Percentage _____   Achieved LTG – YES or NO (circle one)

Discuss your results: (for example: what strategies worked best, what goal difficulties did you encounter, or what did you learn)

_____

_____

_____

Step 7 – If you did not achieve your LTG – Review Strategies and/or STGs and continue to work. Please note that you can modify your strategies and/or STGs at any point during the process.

Space provided for **ST** to review Strategies and review goals (if needed):

_____

_____

_____

_____

Part Two

Student Practice

TASK 8
Feedback to Students

The ability to provide meaningful feedback at just the right time is one of the most important tools that a teacher has (Harrison, Blakemore & Buck, 2000). While there are many types of feedback, specific skill-related feedback is necessary for students who are attempting to learn and/or refine motor skills. Specific skill-related feedback is important because it informs learners about the correctness of their respective movement patterns and gives them information on how to prepare for their next skill attempt. The provision of a teacher's specific skill-related feedback may be especially helpful to beginners who are not able to use the sensory information needed to correctly perform a motor skill (Magill, 1994). Further, many students assume that they are performing a task correctly unless they are told differently (Brophy, 1982).

While it seems logical that feedback could improve student performance, the research in physical education pedagogy does not support the efficacy of feedback (Rink, 1996). Rink (1996) goes on to explain that there is little evidence of a direct linkage between feedback and student learning. Perhaps this finding could be attributed to the limited amount of specific skill related feedback received by physical education students (Fishman & Toby, 1978; Yerg, 1978). Large class sizes with learners at many different skill levels make the delivery of skill-related feedback difficult for teachers. However, a teacher can give skill-related feedback to students by using group corrective feedback when he/she notes many students with the same skill performance error (e.g., many students not achieving side orientation on the overhand throw) (Graham et al., 2001).

The amount and type of feedback students receive is dependent on a classroom's environment and the philosophy of the teacher. Generally, feedback can be directed to a student's skill attempt or to his/her behavior pattern (e.g., a teacher may complement/give positive behavior-related feedback to students' ability to line up quickly and quietly). If most of the feedback given to students is directed to their behavior versus their skill attempts, then the teacher probably has not established an effective classroom structure (see Task 2). Normally behavior-related feedback is delivered in the first couple of weeks of school in order to ensure that students learn to follow class rules and routines. Thereafter, most of the feedback should address skill attempts and be specific-skill related (e.g., transfer your weight to your front foot) as opposed to general feedback (e.g., good throw, nice try) in nature. General feedback can be used as a motivator, but care should be taken not to use too much of this type, since it may devalue the learner if too much is given (Brophy, 1982; Randall, 1992).

Feedback should be given fairly soon after the student's skill attempt, but not too quickly because if the teacher jumps in too soon it may interrupt the student's own assessment. Usually, the teacher should wait about 3-5 seconds after the skill to give the student adequate time to assess his/her own performance (Schmidt, 1991).

So how much feedback is needed for students to effectively learn and/or refine motor skills? Past research has shown that feedback occurs about 3-16% of the time in classroom settings (Seidentop, 1983). A general recommendation for feedback rate is approximately 2 to 3 feedback statements per minute delivered to a class of students. Most (approximately 75%) of these feedback statements should fall under the heading of specific skill-related feedback.

Goal Setting Model for Dealing with this Issue

1. Identify the Issues – Does the **ST/PT** (student teacher/practicing teacher) provide enough feedback (FB) to students? Does the majority of the feedback fall under the specific, skill-related category?

2. Collect Baseline Data – the **ST/PT** can either video or audio tape lessons and then record the number and type of feedback, or the **CT/P** (cooperating teacher/partner) can record the feedback during a class. It would also be helpful if the **ST or CT/ PT or P** recorded the student(s)' gender or group interactions to see if there are any trends that might help the **ST/PT** better monitor their own feedback patterns. For example, maybe males are receiving most of the specific, skill-related feedback and females are receiving more general positive feedback.

Example: 30 minute class

	Female	Male	Group
Positive (Behavior)	1111	11	111111111111
Corrective (Behavior)	11	11111111111	111
Neutral (Behavior)	111	111	0

Calculate Ave. FB for Behavior ___1.3 per min.___   (40 divided by 30 minute class = 1.3)

	Female	Male	Group
General (Skill)	1111111	1111111	111
Specific (Skill)	11111111111	1111111 11111	1111111111

Calculate Ave. FB for Skill ____1.66 per min.____ (50 divided by 30 =1.66)

Calculate Ave. Overall FB ____3.0 per min____ (90 divided by 30 = 3)

Calculate the % of Specific Skill-Related FB ____38%____ 34 / 90 = x/100

3. Set a Specific Goal(s) – set two long term goals (LTG) (one for overall FB rate per minute and one for % of specific, skill-related FB versus general feedback) and/or a series of progressive short term goals (STG) which will lead to the attainment of the long term goals.

For example, LTGs might be to:

Rate per minute: *2 FBs per minute (secondary)*
SUGGESTED Beginning Teacher Standard (BTPS)*
3 FBs per minute (elementary)

% specific skill FB: *75% of FB is specific skill-related*

<u>Note:</u> (*)The "SUGGESTED Beginning Teacher Performance Standard (BTPS)" has been taken from the literature on teacher effectiveness and these standards are strongly suggested for use and appear in BOLD type. While these standards are for the most part achievable, sometimes this standard will need to be adjusted to meet the needs (low SES level of school, large class sizes, etc.) of your teaching situation.

Examples of STGs to achieve a LTG might be to:

Rate per minute:

     .5 FB per minute (secondary)   STG#1
     1 FB per minute (secondary)   STG #2
     2 FBs every minute (secondary)   LTG

     1 FB per minute (elementary)   STG #1
     2 FBs every minute (elementary)   STG #2
     3 FBs every minute (elementary)   LTG

% specific skill-related FB:

     50% of FB is specific skill-related   STG #1
     65% of FB is specific skill-related   STG #2
     75% of FB is specific skill-related   LTG

4.   Outline Specific Strategies to Help **ST/PT** Reach the LTG (Suggested Strategies)

- Focus on giving specific skill-related feedback
- Don't overuse general feedback
- Provide FB to each child
- Focus FB on skill components that you are working on that day (e.g., side orientation in the overhand throw); this is referred to as congruent feedback
- Eliminate the negative in your thoughts and don't use negative FB
- Provide lots of specific FB
- Monitor around the perimeter of the gymnasium or field area and give FB (keeping all students in your line of sight)
- Be energetic and enthusiastic
- Find something positive to say about the skill attempt before giving skill correction
- Do not embarrass students
- Circulate around class to see all students
- Establish classroom structure early in the school year and this will limit the amount of corrective behavior related feedback
- Use group specific FB when many students have the same performance error
- Use peer teaching which allows students to give students FB

5. Collect data to check on the **ST/PT's** progress throughout the week (at least 3-4x at the elementary level and 2x at the secondary level [block or portion of the block schedule])

Example: Class #1 – 30 minute class (elementary)

	Female	Male	Group
Positive (Behavior)	1111 111	11	111111111
Corrective (Behavior)	11	1111111	111
Neutral (Behavior)	0	0	0

Calculate Ave. FB for Behavior ___1.0 per min.___ (30 divided by 30 minute class = 1.0)

	Female	Male	Group
General (Skill)	1111111	111111111111	11111111
Specific (Skill)	11111111111	1111111111111	111111111

Calculate Ave. FB for Skill ___2.2 per min.___ (65 divided by 30 =2.16)

Calculate Ave. Overall FB ___3.2 per min___ (95 divided by 30 = 3.16)

Calculate the % of Specific Skill-related FB ___36%___ 34 / 95 = x/100

Compare these data to your STGs and LTG:

Class #1 (elementary level)

Rate per minute: 3.2   Attained STG #1 (1 FB per min.) & #2 (2 FBs per min.) but not LTG (3 FBs per min.)

% specific skill-related FB: 36%   Not Attained STG #1 (50%)& #2 (65%) or LTG (75%)

Repeat process for the other classes

6. Collect and compare post test data to your LTG

Example: Post test – 30 minute class (elementary)

	Female	Male	Group
Positive (Behavior)	11111	11111	1111111111
Corrective (Behavior)	111	11	0
Neutral (Behavior)	0	0	0

Calculate Ave. FB for Behavior ___.83 per min._____   (25 divided by 30 minute class = .83)

	Female	Male	Group
General (Skill)	11111111	1111111	11111
Specific (Skill)	11111111111111 111111111111111	11111111111111 11111111111111	1111111111 11111

Calculate Ave. FB for Skill ____2.3 per min.____   (70 divided by 30 =2.3)

Calculate Ave. Overall FB ____3.2 per min._____   (95 divided by 30 = 3.16)
Achieved LTG

Calculate the % of Specific Skill-related FB ___79%____   75/95 = x/100
Achieved LTG

7.   If you did not achieve the LTG – revise strategy and/or goal and continue to work toward the LTG with the revisions in place. <u>Note:</u> You can revise your strategies and/or STGs at any point during the process.

TASK 8
Feedback to Students
Systematic Observation Worksheet

ST/PT _____   **School** _____

Date _____

Application of Goal Setting Model

<u>Step 1</u> – Identify Issues – Does the **ST/PT** provide enough feedback (FB) to his/her students? Does the majority of the feedback fall under the category of specific skill-related information?

<u>Step 2</u> – Collect Baseline Data

The **ST/PT** (via video recording) or **CT/P** (using live observation) should complete the following tasks:

1. Count the number of FB occurrences
2. Record this count under the correct category (female, male or group)
3. Total and interpret the data (calculate FB per minute & percentage of specific skill-related FB)

	Females	Males	Group
Positive (Behavior)			
Corrective (Behavior)			
Negative (Behavior)			
General (Skill)			
Specific (Skill)			

Calculate Average FB for Behavior   _____

Calculate Average FB for Skill   _____

Calculate Overall FB per minute   _____

Calculate % of Specific skill-related FB   _____

<u>Step 3</u> – Set Specific LTG and/or Specific STGs – state these in observable terms (e.g., average of FBs per minute, % of Specific Skill-related FBs).

    <u>Note:</u>   The LTG should reflect the Suggested BTPS (for rate per minute).

Feedbacks per minute:

    LTG _____

    STG #1_____

    STG #2_____

% of Specific skill-related FBs:

    LTG _____

    STG #1_____

    STG #2_____

<u>Step 4</u> – List Strategies to Help You Attain your LTG – See "Suggested Strategies" under #4

    1.   _____
         _____

    2.   _____

    3.   _____

    4.   _____

    5.   _____
         _____

Step 5 – Collect data throughout week (3-4x elementary or 2-3x secondary level)

Class   #1   #2   #3   #4   (circle one)

	Females	Males	Group
Positive (Behavior)			
Corrective (Behavior)			
Negative (Behavior)			
General (Skill)			
Specific (Skill)			

Calculate the Ave. FB for Behavior _____
Calculate the Ave. FB for Skill _____

Calculate Overall FB _____
List Goals Achieved: _____

Calculate the % of Specific Skill-related FB _____
List Goals Achieved: _____

Make multiple copies of this page

79

Step 6 – Collect Post Test Data and Compare average to Your LTG

Post Test Class

	Females	Males	Group
Positive (Behavior)			
Corrective (Behavior)			
Negative (Behavior)			
General (Skill)			
Specific (Skill)			

Calculate the Ave. FB for Behavior _____

Calculate the Ave. FB for Skill _____

Calculate Overall FB _____

Did Attain the LTG? YES or NO (circle one)

Calculate the % of Specific Skill-related FB _____

Did Attain the LTG? YES or NO (circle one)

Discuss your results: (for example: what strategies worked best, what goal difficulties did you encounter, or what did you learn)

_____

_____

_____

Step 7 – If you did not achieve your LTG – Review Strategies and/or STGs and continue to work. Please note that you can modify strategies or STGs at any point in this process.

Space provided for **ST/PT** to review Strategies and review goals (if needed):

_____

_____

_____

_____

TASK 9
Time Spent on Teacher Talk

The most important use of time in physical education classes is in the instructional process and in the practice time used by students. In order to increase the amount of time a student spends practicing a sport or fitness related skill, the teacher must plan and implement lessons that minimize time spent on teacher talk time. One way teachers can accomplish this is to keep instructions short and simple (KISS principle) (Graham, et al., 2001). While instructions and information given by teachers are important to the learning process, one must monitor the time devoted to this teacher role to ensure that most of the class time is spent practicing skills or participating in fitness-related activities. The key to minimizing teacher talk time is planning. Teachers need to decide how much information to impart to students. Information about sport skills and fitness activities must be clear and concise (Graham, Hussey, Taylor, & Werner, 1993). For younger learners, a very brief instruction session is needed due to their short attention spans.

Interestingly enough, this issue of too much time spent on teacher talk is not only a common problem of beginning teachers but also a concern for some more experienced teachers (Pangrazi & Darst, 1997). Teachers who talk too much often repeat themselves, give too much biomechanical information, and fail to succinctly state the key components of a skill or fitness task.

When analyzing teacher talk time, it should not include teacher talk related to management activities (e.g., information on how to change stations or transition from one activity to another). Instead, this instructional talk time occurs during the following situations: introduction, skill explanations or fitness activities and demonstrations, extensions, refinements, applications/challenges, directions for culminating activity or lead-up game, and closure.

Teacher talk time is only recorded when students are still, such as standing or sitting while listening to the teacher's instructions, watching skill demonstrations and/or listening to skill analyses. Teacher talk time does not include time when students are moving in a skill or fitness-related activity.

Goal Setting Model for Dealing with this Issue

1. Identify the Issue – measuring the time spent on teacher talk

2. Collect Baseline Data – The **CT/P** (Cooperating teacher/Partner) lists the episodes (e.g., lesson introduction, skill explanation, directions for lead-up game, etc.) where the **ST/PT** (Student teacher / Practicing teacher) is talking (when the students are physically still – e.g., sitting or standing listening to the teacher lecture about a skill or fitness task) and then records the time spent on each task or skill/fitness discussion.

An alternate method of data collection could include making an audio or video recording of the lesson by the **ST/PT**. During a review of this tape, **ST/PT** lists the episodes where he/she is talking and records the time spent on task.

Calculate the percentage of time in teacher talk:

a. List the teacher talk situations (e.g., introduction, skill explanation, etc.) and record the time spent on each task

b. Sum the total amount of time in teacher talk

c. Convert total talk time into seconds (e.g., 1:30 seconds equals 90 seconds)

d. Convert the total amount of time in class into seconds (30 minute class equals 1800 seconds or 60 minute class equals 3600 seconds)

e. Compute a ratio (90/1800 = x /100) to get the percentage management time, in this case x = 5%

Example:

List the talk time situations and the corresponding time

introduction	1 minute
skill explanation	3 minutes
skill extension	5 seconds
lead-up game	3 minutes
closure	1 minute

Sum the total amount of talk time

total time   8:05 min./sec.

Convert management time into seconds

8:05 equals   480 + 5 = 485 seconds

Convert total class time into seconds

30 minute class equals 1800 seconds

Compute percentage

485/1800 = x/100

x = 26.9% of time spent on teacher talk

---

3.   Set a Specific Goal(s) – set a single long term goal (LTG) and/or a series of progressive short term goals (STG) which will lead to the attainment of the long term goal.

For example, a LTG goal might be:

> *15-20% of time spent on teacher talk*
> ***SUGGESTED Beginning Teacher Performance Standard (BTPS)****

<u>Note:</u> (*)The "SUGGESTED Beginning Teacher Performance Standard (BTPS)" has been taken from the literature on teacher effectiveness and these standards are strongly suggested for use and appear in BOLD type. While these standards are for the most part achievable, sometimes this standard will need to be adjusted to meet the needs (low SES level of school, large class sizes, etc.) of your teaching situation.

Examples of STGs to achieve the LTG might be:

> *35-30% of time spent on teacher talk*   (STG #1)
> *29 -25% of time spent on teacher talk*   (STG #2)
> *24-21% of time spent on management tasks*   (STG #3)
> *15-20% of time spent on teacher talk*   (LTG)

4.   Outline Specific Strategies to Help ST Reach LTG (Suggested Strategies)

- Bullet skill components (list skill components and use cue words)
- Use task cards to communicate information
- Prepare these task cards in advance
- Be clear and concise with skill/fitness information
- Do not repeat yourself, but check for understanding through student questioning
- Use brief extensions and applications/challenges
- Chunk information (e.g., all skills have a start – action – stop)
- Use the KISS (Keep It Short and Simple) principle
- Use instant activities
- Use cue words
- Use mental image pictures to help you communicate to your students
- Use visual aids to transmit information to students
- Use the "Teach the Teacher" method to get students to analyze the skill that you are teaching
- Use goal setting for each time segment (e.g., lesson introduction, skill explanation or fitness discussion, explanation of lead-up game or culminating activity, lesson closing). For example, only spend 30 seconds each on the lesson introduction and closing and 1-2 minutes on the skill/fitness explanation.

5.   Collect data to check on the **ST/PT's** progress throughout the week (at least 3-4x at the elementary level and 2-3x at the secondary level [block or portion of the block schedule])

Example: Class #1

List the teacher talk situations and the corresponding time

introduction	20 seconds
skill explanation	3 minutes
check understanding	10 seconds
extension	5 seconds
application	5 seconds
extension	5 seconds
skill explanation	1 minute
refinement	5 seconds
game explanation	1 minute
redirection	1 minute
closure	1 minute

Sum the total amount of talk time

total time 7:50 min./sec.

Convert talk time into seconds

7:50 equals $420 + 50 = 470$ seconds

Convert total class time into seconds

30 minute class equals 1800 seconds

Compute percentage

$470/1800 = x/100$
$x = 26.1\%$ of time spent on talking

Compare these data to your STGs and LTG:

Class #1	
26.1% time on teacher talk	Achieved STG #1 (35-30%) & STG #2 (29-25%) but not STG #3 (24-21%) LTG (15-20%)

Repeat this process for the other classes

6.   Collect and compare post test data to your LTG

Example: Post test class

List teacher talk situations and the corresponding time

introduction	20 seconds
skill explanation	2 minutes
check understanding	10 seconds
extension	5 seconds
application	5 seconds
extension	5 seconds
skill explanation	1 minute
refinement	5 seconds
game explanation	1 minute
redirection	20 seconds
closure	30 seconds

Sum the total amount of teacher talk

total time   5:40 min./sec.

Convert management time into seconds

5:40 equals $300 + 40 = 340$ seconds

Convert total class time into seconds

30 minute class equals 1800 seconds

Compute percentage

$340/1800 = x/100$
$x = 18.8\%$ of time spent on teacher talk

Compare these data to your LTG:

Post test	
18.8% spent on teacher talk	Achieved LTG (15-20%)
ACHIEVED SUGGESTED BTPS (15-20%)	

7. If you did not achieve the LTG – revise strategy and/or STG goal(s) and continue to work towards the LTG with the revisions in place. <u>Note:</u> You can revise your strategies and/or STGs at any point during the process.

TASK 9
Time Spent on Teacher Talk
Systematic Observation Worksheet

ST/PT _____   **School** _____

Date _____

Application of Goal Setting Model

<u>Step 1</u> – Identify Issue – how much time do I spend talking?

<u>Step 2</u> – Collect Baseline Data –The **CT/P** lists teacher talk time situations and then records the time spent on each situation. Or the **ST/PT** can make an audio or video recording and record when teacher talk time episodes occurred and the amount of time spent on each episode.

Calculating the percentage of time in teacher talk requires the following steps:

a. List the teacher talk situations (e.g., introduction, skill explanation, etc.) and record the time spent on each task
b. Sum the total amount of time in teacher talk
c. Convert total talk time into seconds (e.g., 1:30 seconds equals 90 seconds)
d. Convert the total amount of time in class into seconds (30 minute class equals 1800 seconds or 60 minute class equals 3600 seconds)
e. Compute ratio ($90/1800 = x/100$) to get the percentage management time, in this case $x = 5\%$

Base line Data

Teacher Talk Situation	Time Spent Talking
1.	
2.	
3.	
4.	
5.	
6.	
7.	
8.	
9.	
10.	
11.	
12.	
13.	
14.	
15.	
16.	
17.	
18.	
19.	
20.	

Total Time _____

Calculate Time Spent Talking _____

Use the steps a. through e. provided on the previous page to help you make this calculation

Step 3 – Set Specific a LTG and/ or Specific STGs – state these in observable terms
(e.g., percentage of total time spent on teacher talk).

Note: The LTG MUST reflect the Suggested **BTPS**.

Goals related to Teacher Talk:

LTG _____

STG #1_____

STG #2_____

STG #3 _____

<u>Step 4</u> - List Strategies to Help You attain your LTG (lower teacher talk time) – See "Suggested Strategies" under #4.

1. _____
   _____
   _____
2. _____
   _____
3. _____
   _____
4. _____
   _____
5. _____
   _____
   _____

Step 5 – Collect data throughout week (3-4x elementary or 2-3x secondary level)

Class   #1   #2   #3   #4   (circle one)

Teacher Talk Situation	Time Spent Talking
1.	
2.	
3.	
4.	
5.	
6.	
7.	
8.	
9.	
10.	
11.	
12.	
13.	
14.	
15.	
16.	
17.	
18.	
19.	
20.	

Total Time _____

Calculate Percentage of Talk Time _____

Compare Calculated Percentage to Your STGs & LTG:

Percentage _____   List Goal(s) You Achieved _____

Make multiple copies of this page

<u>Step 6</u> – Collect Post Test Data and Compare Calculated Percentage to Your LTG

Post Test Class

Teacher Talk Situation	Time Spent Talking
1.	
2.	
3.	
4.	
5.	
6.	
7.	
8.	
9.	
10.	
11.	
12.	
13.	
14.	
15.	
16.	
17.	
18.	
19.	
20.	

Total Time _____

Calculate Percentage of Talk Time _____

Compare Calculated Percentage to Your LTG:

      Percentage _____   Achieved LTG – YES or NO (circle one)

Discuss your results: (for example: what strategies worked best, what goal difficulties did you encounter, or what did you learn)

_____

_____

_____

Step 7 – If you did not achieve your LTG – Review Strategies and/or STGs and continue to work. Please note that you can modify your strategies and/or STGs at any point during the process.

Space provided for **ST/PT** to review Strategies and review goals (if needed):

_____

_____

_____

_____

Maximizing the time available for students to practice skill and/or fitness activities is the key to effective teaching and student achievement. In order to increase the amount of time a student spends practicing a sport/motor or fitness related skill, the teacher must plan and implement lessons that minimize student wait time. Students can wait in a variety of situations (e.g., waiting in line, waiting for instructions to begin, waiting while teachers deal with disruptive students, waiting to get and return equipment, waiting to take their turn or to practice a skill, waiting during roll call, etc.). Similar to class management and teacher talk time, the key to minimizing student wait time is planning. Teachers can decrease student wait time in the same way they lessen management time by using pre-established routines (e.g., use of signals for getting attention, transition, find a partner, equipment distribution, etc.) to keep the class moving.

Teachers who are not efficient class managers create situations where students spend a lot of time waiting. Unfortunately, this increase in student wait time results, more often than not, in student misbehavior (Siedentop & Tannehill, 2000).

Goal Setting Model for Dealing with this Issue

1.   Identify the Issue – measuring the time spent on student waiting

2.   Collect Baseline Data – The **CT/P** (Cooperating Teacher/Partner) lists wait time situations and then records the time spent on each situation.   This can be done either by tracking individual students or students as a group.

An alternate method of data collection could include making a video recording of the class session by the **ST/PT** (Student Teacher / Practicing Teacher). During a review of this tape, the **ST/PT** lists the episodes where students are waiting and records the time spent on the situation.

Calculating the percentage of student wait time requires the following steps:
a.   List the wait situations and record the time spent on each situation
b.   Sum the total amount of time spent waiting
c.   Convert total management time into seconds (e.g., 1:30 seconds equals 90 seconds)
d.   Convert the total amount of time in class into seconds (30 minute class equals 1800 seconds or 60 minute class equals 3600 seconds)
e.   Compute a ratio ($90/1800 = x/100$) to get the percentage of student wait time, in this case $x = 5\%$

```
Example:

    List the student wait situations and the corresponding time

            roll call            2 minutes (120 seconds)
            line                 15 seconds
            get equipment        1 minute (60 seconds)

    Sum the total amount spent waiting

            total time        3:15 min./sec.

    Convert management time into seconds

            3:15 equals     180 + 15 = 195 seconds

    Convert total class time into seconds

            30 minute class equals  1800 seconds

    Compute percentage

            195/1800 = x/100
            x =  10.83% of time spent on management tasks
```

3. Set a Specific Goal(s) – set a single long term goal (LTG) and/or a series of progressive short term goals (STG) which will lead to the attainment of the long term goal.

    For example, a LTG goal might be:

    ≤20% of time spent on student wait time
    SUGGESTED Beginning Teacher Performance Standard (BTPS)*

Note. *(*)The "SUGGESTED Beginning Teacher Performance Standard (BTPS)" has been taken from the literature on teacher effectiveness and these standards are strongly suggested for use and appear in BOLD type. While these standards are for the most part achievable, sometimes this standard will need to be adjusted to meet the needs (low SES level of school, large class sizes, etc.) of your teaching situation.*

Examples of STGs to achieve the LTG might be:

$\leq 30\%$ of time spent on student wait time	(STG #1)
29-25% of time spent on student wait time	(STG #2)
24-21% of time spent on student wait time	(STG #3)
$\leq 20\%$ of time spent on student wait time	(LTG)

4.   Outline Specific Strategies to Help **ST** Reach LTG (Suggested Strategies)

- Practice routines related to managerial tasks (e.g., attention getting, transitions, etc.)
- Prepare equipment in advance
- Know how you will group students in advance
- If you are using teams – post teams so students know ahead of time
- Use as few transitions as possible
- Use small teams, this increases student practice opportunities and decreases wait time
- Post the day's activities for students to read prior to class
- Complete roll call as students do warm-up exercises
- Use squads with assigned student locations so that the teacher can spot-check student attendance
- Eliminate or decrease the use of lines – if you must use lines, then have many lines with only a few students in each line
- Avoid games that involve waiting in line
- If equipment is not available for every student, have waiting students practice another skill or mentally practice the present skill
- Be creative with equipment (e.g., construct equipment by using lines on the floor as substitute balance beams)
- Limit use of relay activities or use groups with fewer participants
- If equipment is limited, use a peer teaching style so that only half of the students use the equipment
- If equipment is limited, use a stations format with different equipment at each station

5.   Collect data to check on the **ST/PT's** progress throughout the week (at least 3-4x at the elementary level and 2-3x at the secondary level [block or portion of the block schedule])

Example: Class #1

     List student wait time situations and the corresponding time

roll call	2 minutes
get attention	15 seconds
line	1 minute
equipment dist.	1 minute
get a turn	45 seconds
disruptive student	25 seconds
get attention	15 seconds
collect equipment	1 minute

     Sum the total amount of management time

        total time   6:40 min./sec.

     Convert management time into seconds

        6:40 equals   360 + 40 = 400 seconds

     Convert total class time into seconds

        30 minute class equals 1800 seconds

     Compute percentage

        400/1800 = x/100
        x = 22.2% of time spent on management tasks

Compare these data to your STGs and LTG:

Class #1

22.2% time on management tasks   Achieved STG #1 ($\leq$30%), STG #2 (29-25%) & STG #3 (24-21%) but not LTG ($\leq$20%)

Repeat this process for the other classes

6.   Collect and compare post test data to your LTG

Example: Post test class

List student wait time situations and the corresponding time

roll call	1:30 minutes
get attention	15 seconds
line	1 minute
equipment dist.	1 minute
line	15 seconds
switch stations	15 seconds
get attention	15 seconds
switch stations	15 seconds
disruptive student	15 seconds
collect equipment	45 minute

Sum the total amount of student wait time

total time   5:45 min./sec.

Convert wait time into seconds

5:45 equals $300 + 45 = 345$ seconds

Convert total class time into seconds

30 minute class equals 1800 seconds

Compute ratio

$345/1800 = x/100$
$x = 19.2\%$ of time spent on student waiting

Compare these data to your LTG:

Post test

19.2% spent on management   Achieved LTG ($\leq 20\%$)

ACHIEVED SUGGESTED BTPS ($\leq 20\%$)

7. If you did not achieve the LTG – revise strategy and/or STG goal(s) and continue to work toward the LTG with the revisions in place. <u>Note</u>. You can revise your strategies and/or STGs at any point during the process.

TASK 10
Time Spent on Student Waiting
Systematic Observation Worksheet

ST/PT _____   **School** _____
Date _____

Application of Goal Setting Model

Step 1 – Identify Issue – how much time do my students spend waiting?

Step 2 – Collect Baseline Data –The **CT/P** lists wait time situations and then records the time spent on each situation. An alternate method of data collection could include the **ST/PT** making a video recording of the lesson. During a review of this tape, The **ST/PT** lists the episodes where students are waiting and records the time spent on situation.

Calculating the percentage of time spent waiting requires the following steps:
a. List wait time situations and record the time spent on each situation
b. Sum the total amount of time spent waiting
c. Convert total wait time into seconds (e.g., 1:30 min/sec equals 90 seconds)
d. Convert the total amount of time in class into seconds (30 minute class equals 1800 seconds or 60 minute class equals 3600 seconds)
e. Compute a ratio (90/1800 = x /100) to get the percentage of student wait time, in this case x = 5%

Base line Data

Wait Time Situation	Time Spent on Student Waiting
1.	
2.	
3.	
4.	
5.	
6.	
7.	
8.	
9.	
10.	
11.	
12.	
13.	
14.	
15.	

Total Time _____

Calculate Time Spent on Waiting _____

Use the steps a. through e. provided on the previous page to help you make this calculation

Step 3 – Set Specific a LTG and/or Specific STGs – state these in observable terms
   (e.g., percentage of total time spent on student waiting).

  Note. The LTG should reflect the Suggested BTPS.

Goals related to Time Spent on Student Waiting:

  LTG _____

  STG #1_____

  STG #2_____

  STG #3 _____

Step 4 – List Strategies to Help You attain your LTGs (low student wait time) – See
   "Suggested Strategies" under #4.

  1. _____
    _____
    _____
  2. _____
    _____
  3. _____
    _____
  4. _____
    _____
  5. _____
    _____

<u>Step 5</u> – Collect data throughout week (3-4x elementary or 2-3x secondary level)

Class   #1   #2   #3   #4   (circle one)

Wait Time Situation	Time Spent on Student Waiting
1.	
2.	
3.	
4.	
5.	
6.	
7.	
8.	
9.	
10	
11.	
12.	
13.	
14.	
15.	

Total Time _____

Calculate Percentage of Wait Time _____

Compare Calculated Percentage to Your STGs & LTG:

Percentage _____   List Goal(s) You Achieved _____

Make multiple copies of this page

<u>Step 6</u> – Collect Post Test Data and Compare Calculated Percentage to Your LTG

Post Test Class

Wait Time Situation	Time Spent on Student Waiting
1.	
2.	
3.	
4.	
5.	
6.	
7.	
8.	
9.	
10	
11.	
12.	
13.	
14.	
15.	

Total Time _____

Calculate Percentage of Wait Time _____

Compare Calculated Percentage to Your LTG:

Percentage _____   Achieved LTG – YES   or   NO (circle one)

Discuss your results: (for example: what strategies worked best, what goal difficulties did you encounter, or what did you learn)

_____

_____

_____

Step 7 – If you did not achieve your LTG – Review Strategies and/or STGs and continue
to work. Please note that you can modify your strategies and/or STGs at any
point during the process.

Space provided for **ST/PT** to review Strategies and review goals (if needed):

_____

_____

_____

_____

TASK 11
Time Spent on Student Practice

Effective teachers limit time spent in management (Task 7), teacher talk (Task 9) and student waiting (Task 10), in order to provide time for students to practice sport/motor skills and fitness activities. The opportunity for a student to practice skills and/or fitness activities is an important variable controlling learning or achieving an optimal level of performance (Rink, 1996; Schmidt & Wrisberg, 2000). In addition, students cannot become physically fit unless they participate in fitness activities (US Department of Health & Human Services, 1996). Task 11 focuses on student practice opportunities without the element of student success. From a hierarchical viewpoint, teachers must allot student practice time and make sure they are engaged in fitness or motor skill practice before addressing students' successful practice. Task 14 addresses both student motor/fitness engaged with success.

While the opportunity for practice is available to all students, it is the teacher's responsibility to make sure that students take full advantage of this opportunity. Scanning the class, to check for those students who successfully cope and those who avoid the practice opportunity is one way to identify and assist those students to stay on-task and return to the practice situation (Task 4). In addition, teachers should take care to create situations in which students get adequate practice time by seldom creating situations where students must wait for a practice opportunity and use small group/teams that optimize students practice of skill(s) in game situations (e.g., lead-up activities, culminating activities, etc.).

Practice situations are primarily found in the skill and/or fitness development portions of the lesson as well as during the culminating activity or lead-up games. The remaining portions of the lesson are usually devoted to instruction and management activities.

Goal Setting Model for Dealing with this Issue

1. Identify the Issue – measuring the time spent on student practice opportunity

2. Collect Baseline Data – The **CT/P** (cooperating Teacher/Partner) lists the practice opportunity situations where the majority of students are actively engaged in student practice and then records the time spent on each situation.

   An alternate method of data collection could include the **ST/PT** (Student Teacher/Practicing Teacher) making a video recording of the class session. During a review of this tape, the **ST/PT** lists the episodes where students are practicing and records the time spent on situation.

   Still another method of collecting this data could include the **PT** using a stopwatch to record total student practice time and not recording separate situations. This method this would produce a composite time of all practice situations.

Calculating the percentage of time spent in practice requires the following steps:

a.   List the practice situations and record the time spent on each situation

b.   Sum the total amount of time in practice

c.   Convert total practice time into seconds (e.g., 1:30 seconds equals 90 seconds)

d.   Convert the total amount of time in class into seconds (30 minute class equals 1800 seconds or 60 minute class equals 3600 seconds)

e.   Compute a ratio (90/1800 = x /100) to get the percentage practice time, in this case x = 5%

Example:

List the practice situations and the corresponding time

skill practice	2:10 minutes
skill practice	3 minutes
skill practice	3 minutes
game	3 minutes

Sum the total amount of practice time

total time   11:10 min./sec.

Convert management time into seconds

11:10 equals   660 + 10 = 670 seconds

Convert total class time into seconds

30 minute class equals 1800 seconds

Compute percentage

670/1800 = x/100
x = 37.2% of time spent on practice

---

3.   Set Specific Goals – set a single long term goal (LTG) and/or a series of progressive short term goals (STG) which will lead to the attainment of the long term goal.

For example, a LTG goal might be:

> $\geq 50\%$ of time spent on student practice
> **SUGGESTED Beginning Teacher Performance Standard (BTPS)***

Note: (*) The "SUGGESTED Beginning Teacher Performance Standard (BTPS)" has been taken from the literature on teacher effectiveness and these standards are strongly suggested for use and appear in BOLD type. While these standards are for the most part achievable, sometimes this standard will need to be adjusted to meet the needs (low SES level of school, large class sizes, etc.) of your teaching situation.

Examples of STGs to achieve the LTG might be:

$\geq 35\%$ of time spent on student practice	(STG #1)
36-49% of time spent on student practice	(STG #2)
$\geq 50\%$ of time spent on student practice	(LTG)

4.   Outline Specific Strategies to Help **ST** reach LTG (Suggested Strategies)

- Practice routines related to managerial tasks (e.g., attention getting, transitions, etc.) to reduce managerial time
- Prepare equipment in advance
- Know how you will group students in advance
- If you are using teams – post teams so students know ahead of time
- Use few transitions
- Post the day's activities for students to read prior to class
- Complete roll call as students are doing warm-up exercises
- Constantly scan and redirect student who are off-task
- Eliminate lines or use many lines with only a few students per line
- Use enough equipment so that every student has his/her own equipment
- Use challenges and extensions to motivate students
- Design simple to complex skill progressions
- Keep the class moving
- Plan for quick and smooth transitions
- Deal with individual student issues after getting the rest of the class into activity and then deal with the issue
- Place colored numbers on the floor to assist elementary students in quickly finding a "good" personal space or use these numbers to quickly get students into groups/teams
- If equipment is limited, use a peer teaching style so that only half of the students use the equipment at one time, the use of this teaching style would require the teacher to re-define "student practice" to include those students who are actively engaged in peer teaching responsibilities
- If equipment is limited, use a stations format with different equipment at each station

107

5. Collect data to check on the **ST/PT's** progress throughout the week (at least 3-4x at the elementary level and 2-3x at the secondary level [block or portion of the block schedule])

Example: Class #1

 List the practice situations and corresponding time

drill	1:30 minute
skill practice	3 minutes
skill practice	1 minute
skill practice	1 minute
skill practice	30 seconds
mini-game	4:30 minutes

 Sum the total amount of practice time

  total time 11:30 min./sec.

 Convert practice time into seconds

  11:30 equals $660 + 30 = 690$ seconds

 Convert total class time into seconds

  30 minutes class equals 1800 seconds

 Compute percentage

  $690/1800 = x/100$
  $x = 38.3\%$ of time spent on practice

Compare these data to your STGs and LTG:

Class #1

38.3% time on practicing Achieved STG #1 ($\geq$35%) & STG #2 (36-49%) but not LTG ($\geq$50%)

Repeat this process for the other classes

6.   Collect and compare post test data to your LTG

Example: Post test class

List the practice situations and corresponding time

drill	1 minute
skill practice	3 minutes
skill practice	2 minutes
skill practice	2:40 minutes
skill practice	2 minutes
mini-game	4:30 minutes

Sum the total amount of practice time

total time   15:10 min./sec.

Convert practice time into seconds

15:00 equals   900 + 10 = 910 seconds

Convert total class time into seconds

30 minute class equals 1800 seconds

Compute percentage

910/1800 = x/100
x = 50.5% of time spent on practice

Compare these data to your LTG:

Post test

50.5% spent on practice time   Achieved LTG ($\geq$ 50%)

ACHIEVED SUGGESTED BTPS

7.   If you did not achieve the LTG – revise strategy and/or STG goal(s) and continue to work toward the LTG with the revisions in place. <u>Note</u>. You can revise your strategies and/or STGs at any point during the process.

TASK 11
Time Spent on Student Practice
Systematic Observation Worksheet

ST/PT _____   School _____

Date _____

Application of Goal Setting Model

Step 1 – Identify Issue – how much time do I allot for student practice?

Step 2 – Collect Baseline Data –The **CT** lists the practice situations where the majority of students are actively engaged in student practice and then records the time spent on each situation. An alternate method of data collection could include the **ST/PT** making a video recording of the lesson. During a review of this tape, the **ST/PT** lists the episodes where students are practicing and records the time spent on the situation. In addition, the **PT** could use a stopwatch to record student practice time and not record separate situations, just record a total time.

Calculating the percentage of time spent in practice requires the following steps:
a.   List the practice situations and record the time spent on each situation
b.   Sum the total amount of time in practice
c.   Convert total practice time into seconds (e.g., 1:30 seconds equals 90 seconds)
d.   Convert the total amount of time in class into seconds (30 minute class equals 1800 seconds or 60 minute class equals 3600 seconds)
e.   Compute a ratio (90/1800 = x /100) to get the percentage practice time, in this case x = 5%

Baseline Data

Practice Situations	Time Spent on Student Practice
1.	
2.	
3.	
4.	
5.	
6.	
7.	
8.	
9.	
10	
11.	
12.	
13.	
14.	
15.	

Total Time _____

Calculate Time Spent on Student Practice _____

Use steps a. through e. provided on the previous page to help you make this calculation

Step 3 – Set Specific a LTG and/or Specific STGs – state these in observable terms
  (e.g., percentage of total time spent on student practice opportunity).

  Note.   The LTG should reflect the Suggested BTPS.

Goals related to Time Spent on Student Practice Opportunity:

  LTG _____

  STG #1_____

  STG #2_____

  STG #3 _____

Step 4 - List Strategies to Help You attain your LTGs (high student practice time) – See
  "Suggested Strategies" under #4.

  1.   _____
       _____
       _____
  2.   _____
       _____
  3.   _____
       _____
  4.   _____
       _____
  5.   _____
       _____

Step 5 – Collect data throughout week (3-4x elementary or 2-3x secondary level)

Class   #1   #2   #3   #4   (circle one)

Practice Situations	Time Spent on Student Practice
1.	
2.	
3.	
4.	
5.	
6.	
7.	
8.	
9.	
10	
11.	
12.	
13.	
14.	
15.	

Total Time _____

Calculate Percentage of Student Practice Opportunity _____

Compare Calculated Percentage to Your STGs & LTG:

Percentage _____   List Goal(s) You Achieved _____

Make multiple copies of this page

<u>Step 6</u> – Collect Post Test Data and Compare Calculated Percentage to Your LTG

Post Test Class

Practice Situations	Time Spent on Student Practice
1.	
2.	
3.	
4.	
5.	
6.	
7.	
8.	
9.	
10	
11.	
12.	
13.	
14.	
15.	

Total Time _____

Calculate Percentage of Student Practice Opportunity _____

Compare Calculated Percentage to Your LTG:

Percentage _____   Achieved LTG – YES or NO (circle one)

Discuss your results: (for example: what strategies worked best, what goal difficulties did you encounter, or what did you learn)

_____

_____

_____

<u>Step 7</u> – If you did not achieve your LTG – Review Strategies and/or STGs and continue to work. Please note that you can modify your strategies and/or STGs at any point during the process.

Space provided for **ST/PT** to review Strategies and review goals (if needed):

_____

_____

_____

_____

Part Three

Student Practice with Success

TASK 12
How to Individualize Lessons: A Way to Increase Student Success

One way to increase student success is through the individualization of lessons. Students come to their physical education class with a variety of skills and talents. An effective teacher realizes that each student is unique and plans accordingly. The purpose of Task 12 is to help teachers identify modifications to motor skills or fitness activities that may increase student success. Task 13 is an extension of Task 12. In Task 13, the teacher utilizes the planned modifications identified in Task 12 and checks off the modifications actually utilized in the teaching episode/class.

In physical education, a student's skill level is an important factor to consider when planning and implementing lessons. Therefore, when planning to teach sports skills and fitness activities, it is necessary to be able to classify students according to their skill levels. This can be accomplished by using Stanley's (1977) "Generic Levels of Skill Proficiency" which was modified by Graham et al. (2001). The use of this system allows teachers to match an activity or skill to the student's level of proficiency. Briefly, this system of skill classification has 4 levels: (a) precontrol (beginner) – where a student cannot replicate a movement pattern, (b) control (advanced beginner) – where the movement is more consistent and repetitions are more similar in appearance, (c) utilization (intermediate) – movements are more automatic and successful; with students able to deal with predictable changes related to the skill, and (d) proficiency (advanced) – movements are automatic and student can deal with unpredictable skill situations (Graham et al., 2001). For a more detailed discussion of the "Generic Levels of Skill Proficiency," review Graham's et al. (2001) discussion in chapter seven of his book. Further, a summary of this classification system, found in Graham's et al. (2001) book, is located in Table 1 of this book (see page 119).

When planning for all students, teachers must give consideration to those students with special needs. This planning process must address the students' needs and make accommodations to modify existing classroom activities where needed. Teachers should be aware of the student's IEP (Individualized Education Program) and work with parents and special education teachers to ensure the student's safe and productive inclusion into your class. Awareness of the IEP's contraindicated exercise(s) and/or activity(ies) will also help you plan an appropriate instructional intervention for these students. Many books and articles have been written on successful inclusion strategies for students with special needs (see Block, 1994 for an example of these inclusion strategies). However, the same levels of skill proficiency also apply to this population.

During the planning process, skill/fitness modifications can be delivered through three primary sources: (a) extending tasks – making the task/activity easier or more difficult depending on the student's skill/fitness level or need, (b) challenges –motivational tests/questions or applications to the skill/fitness activity and (c) refinement – cues or critical elements that will assist them in becoming more proficient (Graham et al., 2001; Rink, 1993).

Not only are students different from one another, they are also different with respect to different skills. Just because a student is proficient in the forehand drive in tennis does not mean that he/she is proficient when dribbling a soccer ball or even on serving a tennis ball.

The teacher's ability to adapt skill/fitness tasks to meet the needs of all students is the mark of an effective teacher. Whether this is accomplished through extensions, challenges or refinements, all of these elements help the teacher to individualize instruction so that all students can achieve.

Table 1

Observable Characteristics of the Generic Levels of Skill Proficiency

Precontrol Level (Beginner)

- Student is unable to repeat movements in succession; one attempt does not look like another attempt to perform the same movement.
- Student uses extraneous movements that are unnecessary for proficiently performing the skill.
- Student seems awkward and doesn't even come close to performing the skill correctly.
- Correct performances are characterized more by surprise than by expectancy.
- When a student practices with a ball, the ball seems to control the student.

Control Level (Advanced Beginner)

- The student's movements appear less haphazard and seem to conform more to the student's intentions.
- Movements appear more consistent, and repetitions are somewhat alike.
- The student begins to perform the skill correctly more frequently.
- The student's attempt to combine one movement with another or perform the skill in relation to an unpredictable object or person is usually unsuccessful.
- Because the movement isn't automatic, the student needs to concentrate intensely on what he or she is doing.

Utilization Level (Intermediate)

- The movement becomes more automatic and can be performed successfully with concentration.
- Even when the context of the task is varied (slightly at first), the student can still perform the movement successfully.
- The student has developed control of the skill in predictable situations and is beginning to move skillfully in unpredictable situations. The student can execute the skill the same way consistently.
- The student can use the skill in combination with other skills and still perform it appropriately.

Proficiency Level (Advanced)

- The skill has become almost automatic, and performances in a similar context appear almost identical.
- The student is able to focus on extraneous variables – an opponent, an unpredictable object, the flow of travel – and still perform the skill as intended.
- The movement often seems effortless as the student performs the skill with ease and seeming lack of attention.
- The movement can be performed successfully in a variety of planned and unplanned situations as the student appears to modify performance to meet the demands of the situation.

Table taken from:

Graham, G., Holt/Hale, S.A., & Parker, M. (2001). *Children moving: A reflective approach to teaching children physical education.* (5th ed.). (p. 95). Mountain View, CA: Mayfield.

Table in Graham et al. (2001) adapted from the work of:

Stanley, S. (1997). *Physical education: A movement orientation* (2nd ed.). New York: McGraw Hill.

Goal Setting Model for Dealing with this Planning Issue

1.   Identify the Issue – planning for all of your students with differing skill and fitness levels as well as students with special needs

2.   Collect Baseline Data – <u>Phase One</u> – The **ST/PT** (Student Teacher/Practicing Teacher) will either directly observe or videotape his/her classes and classify students' skill levels using the "Generic Levels of Skill Proficiency." These levels of skill proficiency can also be used to classify students with special needs. A summary of these generic skill levels is given on page 119. Further, in a fitness or skill-related lesson the **ST/PT** will need to find out their students' fitness or skill levels and plan modifications to the lesson accordingly. One way to ascertain a student's fitness level is by reviewing students' resting heart rates as a rough indicator of their respective fitness levels or by examining your students' cardiovascular fitness is to examine their one-mile run times. Skill levels can be determined by placing students in game-like situation and applying the "Generic Levels of Skill Proficiency." <u>Phase Two</u> – Once students have been classified (e.g., precontrol through proficiency skill level or low to high fitness), then the **ST/PT** will need to list all variations (extensions, challenges and refinement targeted to students of differing skill/fitness levels and student(s) with special needs [SSN]) in their lesson plan/outline.

Example: Lesson Focus – Dribbling a basketball (Mrs. Brown's 3rd grade class)

Phase One: List students and classify them into skill levels:

Name	Skill Level
John	Control
Susan	Utilization
Mark	Precontrol
Amy (SSN)	Precontrol
Marcus	Control
Linda	Control
etc.	

Phase Two: List skill variations for each skill level:
- precontrol - extension (eyes down)
- control - extension (eyes up)
- utilization - challenge (eyes up – 10 sec.)
- SSN – refinement (stationary)
- precontrol - refinement (wrist action)
- SSN/precontrol - extension (pathway)
- control - challenge (eyes up – 5 sec.)
- utilization - extension (pathway)
- control - extension (moving & levels)
- SSN - challenge (moving)

3.   Set a Specific Goal(s) – set a single long term goal (LTG) and/or a series of progressive short term goals (STG) which will lead to the attainment of the long term goal.

For example, a LTG goal might be to:

> Complete this task for 100% of your classes and all students across skill and/or fitness levels.

Examples of STGs to achieve the LTG might be to:

Complete this task for 50% of your classes/activities	STG #1
Complete this task for 75% of your classes/activities	STG #2
Complete this task for 100% of your classes/activities	LTG

4.   Outline Specific Strategies to Help **ST** Reach LTG (Suggested Strategies)

- Know the variations (Extension, Challenges & Refinements) for each skill you plan to use and place these into your LP
- Consult resources (Block, 1994; Darst & Pangrazi, 2002; Graham, Holt/Hale & Parker, 1998; Graham, et. al.. 2001; Holt/Hale, 2001;Pangrazi & Dauer, 1995; Rink, 1993; plus the Steps to Success Series – e.g., Owens & Bunker,1989; Viera,& Ferguson, 1989) to help you develop appropriate task variations (extensions, challenges and refinements)
- Start with one skill or fitness activity and complete the two phases and then move to the next set of tasks until all classes and students' lessons are individualized
- Work with **CT/P** or special education teacher to plan appropriate variations for SSN
- Write the variations for each skill or fitness level down on a note card or lesson plan
- **CT** can check for individualization in **ST's** lesson plans and note where lessons/activities were modified to account for individual differences

5.   Collect data to check on the **ST/PT's** Progress – check-off the classes where this planning process has been applied to create individualized lessons for students of all skill and fitness levels.

Example: Class #1 – Lesson Focus – Dribbling a basketball (6th grade – Mr. Jones' class)

Phase One: List students and classify them into skill levels:

Name	Skill Level
Harry	Control
Steve	Utilization
Martha	Precontrol
Andrew(SSN)	Control
Mary	Control
Luke	Control
etc.	

Phase Two: List skill variations for each skill level:

- control - extension (including force)
- control - challenge (number of times)
- SSN - extension (stationary dribble)
- SSN – refinement (fingerpads)
- precontrol – extension (pathways)
- SSN - extension (pathway)
- control – extension (inc. force)
- utilization - challenge (eyes up – 20 sec.)
- utilization - extension (moving)
- SSN – extension (non-dominant hand)

Example: Class #1 – Lesson Focus – Fitness activities (cardiovascular, flexibility, muscular strength and endurance) (7th grade – Mr. Jones' class)

Phase One: List students and classify them into fitness levels:

Name	Fitness Level
Julie	High
Susan	Medium
Martha	Low
Andrew(SSN)	Low
Mary	Medium
Luke	High
etc.	

Phase Two: List skill variations for each fitness level:

3.   low, medium & high – weights adjusted for students – extension
4.   low – fewer repetitions required to complete station – challenge
5.   SSN/low – verbal instead of written instructions – extension
6.   medium & high – jog to next station and jog in place until given the signal to begin – extension
7.   high – more repetitions at a faster pace needed to complete the station – extension
etc.

Calculate the percent of classes that have been individualized:

Mr. Jones teaches 6th, 7th and 8th grade classes (2 at each grade level) taught on a block schedule. If he completed the individualization process for the 6th and 7th graders then he would be 2/3 (66%) done with this process.

Compare these data to your STGs and LTG:

Class #1

66% of classes completed   Achieved STG #1 (50%)
                                  but not STG #2 (75%) or
                                  LTG (100%)

6.   Collect and compare post test data to your LTG

Example: 8th grade class – Lesson Focus – Fitness activities (cardiovascular, flexibility, muscular strength and endurance)

Phase One: List students and classify them into fitness levels:

   Name   Fitness Level

   Julie   High
   Susan   Medium
   etc.

Phase Two: List skill variations for each fitness level:

   1.   low, medium & high – weights adjusted for students – extension
   2.   low – can you complete 3 repetitions – challenge etc.

****

Example: 6th and 7th grade classes – Lesson Focus – Dribbling a basketball

Phase One: List students and classify them into skill levels:

   Name   Skill Level

   Harry   Control
   Steve   Utilization
   Martha   Precontrol
   Andrew (SSN)   Control
   etc.

Phase Two: List skill variations for each skill level:

   – control - extension (inc. force)
   – control - challenge (No. of times)
   – SSN - extension (stationary dribble)
   – SSN – refinement (fingerpads)

LTG achieved (100% of classes were individualized)

7. If you did not achieve the LTG – revise strategy and/or goal and continue to work toward the LTG with the revisions in place. <u>Note:</u> You can revise your strategies and/or STGs at any point during the process.

TASK 12
How to Individualize Lessons: A Way to Increase Student Success
Systematic Observation Worksheet

ST/PT_____   School _____

Date _____

Application of Goal Setting Model

Step 1 – Identify Issue – planning needed to individualize lessons for all students.

Step 2 – Collect Baseline Data – Phase One – The **ST/PT** will observe or videotape his/her classes and classify students' skill levels using the "Generic Levels of Skill Proficiency." A summary of these generic skill levels is given on page 119. Further, in a fitness lesson the **ST/PT** will need to find out their students' fitness levels and plan modifications to the lesson accordingly. Phase Two – Once students have been classified (e.g., precontrol through proficiency level or low to high fitness), then the **ST/PT** will need to list all variations (extensions [E], challenges [C] and refinement [R] targeted to students of differing skill/fitness levels and student(s) with special needs [SSN]) in the lesson plan/outline.

Grade/Class _____   Skill/Fitness Activity Focus_____

Phase One – Classification of Students into Skill/Fitness Levels

Student Names	Classification of Students (Skill or Fitness Level)
1.	
2.	
3.	
4.	
5.	
6.	
7.	
8.	
9.	
10.	
11.	
12.	
13.	
14.	
15.	
16.	
17.	
18.	

Phase Two – List variations for students of differing skill or fitness levels.

Skill or Fitness Classification	List Variation & Type (E, C, or R)
1.	
2.	
3.	
4.	
5.	
6.	
7.	
8.	
9.	
10.	
11.	
12.	
13.	
14.	
15.	
16.	
17.	
18.	

Make as many copies as needed since individual activities (e.g., in a basketball lesson you might cover the following skills --- dribbling, passes, shooting skills, etc.) because all of these skill classifications (phase one) and variations (phase two) would need to be completed for each class.

Step 3 – Set Specific a LTG and/ or Specific STGs – state these in observable terms (e.g., percent of individualization completed).

LTG _____

STG #1_____

STG #2_____

Step 4 - List Strategies to Help You attain your LTGs – See "Suggested Strategies" under #4.

1. _____

2. _____

3. _____

4. _____

5. _____

Step 5 – Collect data throughout week with individual activities within classes.

Grade/Class _____ Skill/Fitness Activity Focus_____

Phase One – Classification of Students into Skill/Fitness Levels

Student Names	Classification of Students (Skill or Fitness Level)
1.	
2.	
3.	
4.	
5.	
6.	
7.	
8.	
9.	
10.	
11.	
12.	
13.	
14.	
15.	
16.	
17.	
18.	

Phase Two – List variations for students of differing skill or fitness levels.

Skill or Fitness Classification	List Variation & Type (E, C, or R)
1.	
2.	
3.	
4.	
5.	
6.	
7.	
8.	
9.	
10.	
11.	
12.	
13.	
14.	
15.	
16.	
17.	
18.	

Make as many copies as needed since individual skill or fitness activities will need to be completed for each class.

Calculate % lesson and activities individualized _____

Compare Percent to Your STGs & LTG:

Percentage _____   List Goal(s) You Achieved _____

– Collect Post Test Data and Compare average to Your LTG

Grade/Class _____ Skill/Fitness Activity Focus_____

Phase One – Classification of Students into Skill/Fitness Levels

Student Names	Classification of Students (Skill or Fitness Level)
1.	
2.	
3.	
4.	
5.	
6.	
7.	
8.	
9.	
10.	
11.	
12.	
13.	
14.	
15.	
16.	
17.	
18.	

<u>Phase Two</u> – List variations for students of differing skill or fitness levels.

Skill or Fitness Classification	List Variation & Type (E, C, or R)
1.	
2.	
3.	
4.	
5.	
6.	
7.	
8.	
9.	
10.	
11.	
12.	
13.	
14.	
15.	
16.	
17.	
18.	

Make as many copies as needed since individual skill or fitness activities will need to be completed for each class.

Calculate % of lesson and activities within lesson that you individualized

_____

Compare Calculated Percentage to Your LTG:

Percentage _____   Achieved LTG – YES   or   NO   (circle one)

Discuss your results: (for example: what strategies worked best, what goal difficulties did you encounter, or what did you learn)

_____

_____

_____

Step 7 – If you did not achieve your LTG – Review Strategies and/or STGs and continue to work. Please note that you can modify your strategies and/or STGs at any point during the process.

Space provided for **ST/PT** to review Strategies and review goals (if needed):

_____

_____

_____

_____

TASK 13
Individualizing Lessons: A Way to Increase Student Success

One way to increase student success is by implementing teaching elements (extensions, challenges and refinements) that individualize lessons. An effective teacher realizes that each student is unique and acts according to his/her individual needs.

In Task 12, the "Generic Levels of Skill Proficiency" proposed by Stanley (1977) and modified by Graham et al. (1998) were used as a framework for individualizing instruction. The use of these levels to classify students into skill proficiency categories is important to consider when planning and implementing lessons. Briefly, this system of skill classification has four levels: (1) precontrol (beginner) – where a student cannot replicate a movement pattern; (2) control (advanced beginner) – where the movement is more consistent and repetitions are more similar in appearance; (3) utilization (intermediate) – movements are more automatic and successful but student can deal with predictable changes related to the skill and (4) proficiency (advanced) – movements are automatic and student can deal with unpredictable skill situations (Graham et al., 1998). For a more detailed discussion of the "Generic Levels of Skill Proficiency," review Graham's et al. (1998) discussion in chapter seven of his book. Further, a summary of these skill levels is located on page 119 in Task 12. In addition to students' skill levels, the teacher must consider students' fitness levels (high to low) in order to individualize fitness activities. Students can be categorized within low to high fitness levels based on fitness test scores and/or resting heart rates.

When planning for all students, teachers must also consider students with special needs. This planning must address the student's needs and make accommodations to modify existing classroom activities where needed. Teachers should be aware of the student's IEP (Individualized Education Program) and work with the parents and special education teachers to ensure the student's safe and productive inclusion in the class environment.

Two strategies that allow teachers to adjust for individual differences are (a) teaching by invitation and (b) intratask variation (Graham, et al., 2002). Teaching by invitation involves an invitation offered by the teacher to try a modification (extension) on a skill (e.g., "When you are ready, try to look up when dribbling the ball. This will allow you to move around more safely."). In this strategy, the student decides when to accept the teacher's invitation to try the skill modification (extension). In contrast, intratask variation does not allow students to decide on whether or not they will accept the invitation; instead the teacher designates which students will try the skill modification (extension and/or challenge). For example, the teacher may say, "Tom, Susie and Ann try to dribble the ball while looking up."

Modifications to skills can be delivered in three ways: (a) extending (E) tasks – by making the task/activity easier or harder depending on the student's skill level or need, (b) challenges (C) – by providing motivational tests/questions or applications to the skill and (c) refinement (R) – by providing cues or critical elements that will assist students to become more proficient (Graham et al. 1998; Rink, 1993).

Goal Setting Model for Dealing with this Issue

1. Identify the Issue – inability of **ST/PT** (Student Teacher/Practicing Teacher) to implement variations/modifications found in lesson plan in the actual lesson

2. Collect Baseline Data – The **ST/PT** lists all planned modifications (extensions [E], challenges [C] and refinements [R] targeted to students of differing skill levels and students with special needs [SSN]) found in their lesson plan. These modifications can be delivered either by intratask variation or by teaching by invitation. The **CT/P** (Cooperating Teacher/Partner) simply checks to see if the **ST/PT** covered these in the actual lesson. An alternative data gathering method would require the **ST/PT** first to list all of the planned individualization incidences given in the lesson plan and then videotape his/her lesson and check off the Es, Cs, & Rs when these occurred in the lesson.

Example: Dribbling

Variations	Check off
– precontrol - extension (eyes down)	X
– control - extension (eyes up)	
– utilization - challenge (eyes up – 10 sec.)	X
– SSN – refinement (stationary)	X
– precontrol - refinement (wrist action)	
– SSN - extension (pathway)	X
– control - challenge (eyes up – 5 sec.)	
– utilization - extension (pathway)	X
– control - extension (moving & levels)	
– SSN - challenge (moving)	X

Calculate % of checked incidences to total number of variations – 60%

---

3. Set a Specific Goal(s) – set a single long term goal (LTG) and/or a series of progressive short term goals (STGs) which will lead to the attainment of the long term goal.

    For example, a LTG goal might be:

100% match between lesson plan variations (LPV) and those observed in actual lesson (AL)

Examples of STGs to achieve the LTG might be:

50-74% match between LPV & those observed in AL	STG #1
75-99% match between LVP & those observed in AL	STG #2
100% match between LVP & those observed in AL	LTG

4. Outline Specific Strategies to Help **ST** Reach LTG (Suggested Strategies)

- Know the variations you used in the your LP
- Use teaching by invitation or intratask variation to deliver extension, challenges and refinements to the targeted students
- Plan ahead and designate equipment or groups that would pre-identify students at different skill levels (e.g., "all students with red hockey sticks do this ..." [control students])
- Work with CT to plan appropriate variations for SSN
- If you can not remember the variations, then write them down on a note card and use it
- Plan ahead – know how to make each activity or skill easier or harder (extensions)

5. Collect data to check on the **ST's** Progress– throughout the week (at least 3-4x at the elementary level and 2-3x at the secondary level [block or portion of the block schedule])

Example: Class #1 – dribbling lesson	
Variations	Check off
– control - extension (including force)	X
– control - challenge (Number of times)	X
– SSN - extension (stationary dribble)	X
– SSN – refinement (fingerpads)	
– precontrol – extension (pathways)	X
– SSN - extension (pathway)	X
– control – extension (inc. force)	
– utilization - challenge (eyes up – 20 sec.)	X
– utilization - extension (moving)	
– SSN – extension (non-dominant hand)	X

Calculate % of check off incidences to total number of variations – 70% $(7/10 = x/100)$

Compare these data to your STGs and LTG:

Class #1

70% match between LPV & those observed in AC   Achieved STG #1 (50-74%)
                                              but not STG #2 (75-99%) or
                                              LTG (100%)

Repeat process for the other classes

6.   Collect and compare post test data to your LTG

Example: Post test class

Variations	Check off
– precontrol - extension (eyes down)	X
– control - extension (eyes up)	X
– utilization - challenge (eyes up – 10 sec.)	X
– SSN – refinement (stationary)	X
– precontrol - refinement (wrist action)	X
– SSN - extension (pathway)	X
– control - challenge (eyes up – 5 sec.)	X
– utilization - extension (pathway)	X
– control - extension (moving & levels)	X
– SSN - challenge (moving)	X

Calculate % of check-off incidences to total number of variations –
100%
(10/10=x/100)

Achieved LTG of 100%

7.   If you did not achieve the LTG – revise strategy and/or goal and continue to work
toward the LTG with the revisions in place. **Note:** You can revise your
strategies and/or STGs at any point during the process.

TASK 13
Individualizing Lessons: A Way to Increase Student Success
Systematic Observation Worksheet

ST/PT _____   **School** _____
Date _____

Application of Goal Setting Model

<u>Step 1</u> – Identify Issue – inability of **ST/PT** to implement variations/modifications found in lesson plan into actual lesson

<u>Step 2</u> – Collect Baseline Data – The **ST/PT** lists all modifications (extensions, challenges and refinement targeted to students of differing skill levels and students with special needs [SSN]) found in the lesson plan. **CT/P** simply checks to see if the **ST/PT** covered these in the actual lesson. An alternative data gathering method would require the **ST/PT** first to list all of the planned individualization incidences given in the their lesson plan and then videotape his/her lesson and check off the Es, Cs, & Rs when these occurred in the lesson.

Variations in LP	Check off in AL
1.	
2.	
3.	
4.	
5.	
6.	
7.	
8.	
9.	
10.	
11.	
12.	
13.	
14.	
15.	
16.	
17.	
18.	
19.	
20.	
21.	
22.	
23.	
24.	

Calculate % between LPV & AL _____

Step 3 – Set Specific a LTG and/or Specific STGs – state these in observable terms
(e.g., percent agreement between LPV & AL).

LTG _____

STG #1_____

STG #2_____

Step 4 - List Strategies to Help You attain your LTGs (high percentage of LPV & AL) –
See "Suggested Strategies" under #4.

1. _____
_____

2. _____
_____

3. _____
_____

4. _____
_____

5. _____
_____

Step 5 – Collect data throughout week (3-4x elementary or 2-3x secondary level)

Class   #1   #2   #3   #4   (circle one)

Variations in LP	Check off in AL
1.	
2.	
3.	
4.	
5.	
6.	
7.	
8.	
9.	
10.	
11.	
12.	
13.	
14.	
15.	
16.	
17.	
18.	
19.	
20.	
21.	
22.	
23.	
24.	

Calculate % between LPV & AL _____

Compare Percent to Your STGs & LTG:

Percentage _____   List Goal(s) You Achieved _____

Make multiple copies of this page

Step 6 – Collect Post Test Data and Compare average to Your LTG

Post Test Class

Variations in LP	Check off in AL
1.	
2.	
3.	
4.	
5.	
6.	
7.	
8.	
9.	
10.	
11.	
12.	
13.	
14.	
15.	
16.	
17.	
18.	
19.	
20.	
21.	
22.	
23.	
24.	

Calculate % between LPV & AL _____

Compare Percent to Your LTG:

Percentage _____   Achieved LTG – YES or NO (circle one)

Discuss your results: (for example: what strategies worked best, what goal difficulties did you encounter, or what did you learn)

_____

_____

_____

<u>Step 7</u> – If you did not achieve your LTG – Review Strategies and/or STGs and continue to work. Please note that you can modify your strategies and/or STGs at any point during this process.

Space provided for **ST/PT** to review Strategies and review goals (if needed):

_____

_____

_____

_____

TASK 14
Student Success

The hallmark of a truly effective teacher is the ability to help students achieve success. The accomplishment of this task is extremely difficult and requires a teacher to plan and implement lessons that are individualized with a high percentage of the time devoted to student practice and success over a period of time that is sufficient for the learning of motor skills or the achievement of fitness goals (Goldberger & Gerney, 1990; Metzler, 1989; Silverman, 1990; Silverman & Ramirez, 1991). Teachers must select learning activities that are developmentally appropriate for students' age, skill level and needs. A task that produces about an 80% success rate is one in which students are more likely to continue to participate (Berliner, 1984; 1987; Brophy, 1983; Rosenshine, 1983; Siedentop, 1991). While this notion is strongly supported in the general research education literature, Rink (1996) pointed out that a success rate of 80% free throw shooting in basketball was not really realistic for basketball players of any skill level. However, there are ways that teachers can modify the skill/activity to increase students' level of success (e.g., break the skill into smaller parts, modify the equipment, apply different task requirements for students of differing skill levels, etc). Further, teachers must plan activities that can be delivered at several levels of proficiency by individualizing task extensions, challenges and refinements (cues) for students at different skill or fitness levels. Another way a lesson can be individualized is through the application of Mosston and Ashworth's (1986) inclusion teaching style. This teaching style allows students to select their own level of skill/fitness tasks thereby promoting their success. In addition, the ability to plan instruction in small sequential steps where students can attain success is always a good idea.

Goal Setting Model for Dealing with this Issue

1.   Identify the Problem – gauging student success across skill/fitness activities and handicapping conditions

2.   Collect Baseline Data – the **CT/P** (Cooperating Teacher/Partner) records the number of skill attempts and their success across a variety of skill/fitness levels or handicapping conditions. In order to complete this task the **CT/P** must complete the following steps:
   a.   select 4 students at low (precontrol/beginner or control/advanced beginner), medium (utilization/intermediate) and high (proficiency/advanced) skill levels as well as a student with special needs and record their names at the appropriate category (by skill or SSN line)
   b.   decide on what constitutes success (e.g., fitness activity – full participation, or if you monitor heart rates exercising in the target heart rate zone; skill activity – maybe the **ST/PT** (Student Teacher/Practicing Teacher) may focus on one or two skill components and that would define success for that day), or you may define success differently for the student with special needs (SSN) or students at a low skill or fitness level

c. during the skill and/or fitness activities record the number of skill attempts as well as the number of successful attempts
d. count attempts and successes of student in 1 or 2 minute intervals
e. calculate percent success rate and note the total number of skill/fitness activity attempts

Note 1. The number of skill attempts (across the same number of intervals completed) and rates of success should be similar across skill levels and handicapping conditions.

Note 2. The **ST/PT** and **CT/P** must also decide how to handle skills with continuous movement (e.g., running, dribbling, etc.). A suggested strategy might recommend that the **CT/P** watch the skill for 5 seconds and then decide if the skill attempt was successful.

Example:

Criterion for success: overhand throw with **side orientation for all students**

Intervals (1 or 2 minutes) per student (**CT** selects interval of minutes)

Low skilled student ___John___

1. _1111xxx_

2. _11xxxxx_

3. _1x1x1x1x_

4. _____

5. _____

Total no. of skill attempts __22__
Total no. of successes ___12__
Percent success ___55%__

Medium skilled student ___Mike___

1. ___1111xxxxx

2. ___xxxxxxxxx

3. ___1x1x1x1x1

4. _____

5. _____

Total no. of skill attempts ___27__
Total no. of successes ___18_
Percent success ___67%__

High skilled student ___Ann___
Intervals (1-2 minutes)

1. ___xxxx11111

2. ___xxxxxxxx_

3. ___11xxxxxxxxx_

4. _____

5. _____

Total no. of skill attempts __28__
Total no. of successes __21__
Percent success __75%_

Special needs student ___Barb_

1. ___11111xxx

2. ___xxxxx1111_

3. ___1111xx__

4. _____

5. _____

Total no. of skill attempts ___23__
Total no. of successes __10_
Percent success __43%__

Key = 1 (skill attempt) & x (successful skill attempt)

3.   Set Specific Goals – set a single long term goal (LTG) and/or a series of progressive short term goals (STGs) which will lead to the attainment of the long term goal.

For example, a LTG might be:

> *80% success rate for all students*
> ***SUGGESTED Beginning Teacher Performance Standard (BTPS)****

<u>***Note:***</u> ***(*)The "SUGGESTED Beginning Teacher Performance Standard (BTPS)" has been taken from the literature on teacher effectiveness and these standards are strongly suggested for use and appear in BOLD type. While these standards are for the most part achievable, sometimes this standard will need to be adjusted to meet the needs (low SES level of school, large class sizes, etc.) of your teaching situation.***

Examples of STGs to achieve a LTG might be:

50-64% success rate for all students	(STG #1)
65-79% success rate for all students	(STG #2)
≥80% success rate for all students	(LTG)

4.   Outline Specific Strategies to Help **ST** Reach LTG (Suggested Strategies)

- Plan for success with lots of extensions, challenges & refinements for students at different skill levels and for SSN
- Give students lots of opportunities for practice
- Break skills down into small sequential parts
- Use inclusion teaching style (Mosston & Ashworth, 1986)
- Clearly define the criteria for success
- Group students by ability
- Individualize instruction through extensions, challenges and refinements
- Use reflective teaching to adjust lesson plan to promote student success in the next lesson
- Make adjustments to existing lesson to promote student success
- Pre-test to gauge the students' skill and/or fitness level and plan accordingly
- Modify equipment to make tasks easier or harder for students
- Use different activities or tasks for students of differing skill levels
- If equipment is limited, use a peer teaching style so that only half of the students use the equipment
- If equipment is limited, use a stations format with different equipment at each station

5.　　Collect data to check on the **ST's** progress throughout the week (at least 3-4x at the elementary level and 2-3x at the secondary level [block or portion of the block schedule])

Example:

Criterion for success: overhand throw with **side orientation for all students**

Intervals (1 or 2 minutes) per student (**CT/P** selects interval of minutes)

Low skilled student ___John___	Medium skilled student ___Mike___
1. _1111xxx_	1. _1111xxxxx_
2. _11xxxxx_	2. _xxxxxxxxx_
3. _1x1x1x1x_	3. _1x1x1x1x1_
4.	4.
5.	5.

Total no. of skill attempts _22_		Total no. of skill attempts _27_
Total no. of successes _12_		Total no. of successes _18_
Percent success _55%_		Percent success _67%_

High skilled student ___Ann___ Intervals (1-2 minutes)	Special needs student ___Barb_
1. _xxxx11111_	1. _111xxxxx_
2. _xxxxxxxx_	2. _xxxxx1111_
3. _11xxxxxxxxx_	3. _1111xx_
4.	4.
5.	5.

Total no. of skill attempts _28_		Total no. of skill attempts _23_
Total no. of successes _21_		Total no. of successes _12_
Percent success _75%_		Percent success _52%_

Key = 1 (skill attempt) & x (successful skill attempt)

Class #1	
All levels	Attained STG #1 (50-64%) but not STG #2 (65-79%) or LTG ($\geq$80%)

Repeat process for the other classes

6.   Collect and compare post test data to your LTG

Criterion for success: overhand throw with **side orientation for all students**

Intervals (1 or 2 minutes) per student (**CT** selects interval of minutes)

Low skilled student ___Pat_____   Medium skilled student ___Sue_____

1.__1111x xxxxx xx_____   1.____1111x xxxxx x11xx xxx_____

2.__11xxx xx11x xxxxx x_____   2.____xxxxx xxxx1 1xxx_____

3.___1x1x1 x1xxx xx_____   3.____1x1x1 x1x1x xxxxx xxxx_

4.__xxxx1 11xxx xx_____   4.____1x1x1 x1x_____

5._____   5._____

Total no. of skill attempts __52__   Total no. of skill attempts ____58___
Total no. of successes   __37__   Total no. of successes   ____42__
Percent success   71%_   Percent success   ___72%_

High skilled student ___Harry_____   Special needs student _____Carol___
Intervals (1-2 minutes)

1.____xxxx1 1111x xxxx____   1._____111xx xxx1x xxx_

2.____xxxxx xxxxx xxxxx x   2._____xxxxx 1111x xx___

3.____11xxx xxxxx xxxxx x_   3._____1111x xxxxx_xxxxx_

4.____xxxxx xxxxx xxx___   4._____xxxxx xxxxx_

5._____   5._____

Total no. of skill attempts __59__   Total no. of skill attempts ____50___
Total no. of successes   __51__   Total no. of successes   ____38__
Percent success   86%_   Percent success   ___76%

Key = 1 (skill attempt) & x (successful skill attempt)

Did not Achieve LTG (≥80%) across all groups

7.   If you did not achieve the LTG – revise strategy and/or goal and continue to work toward the LTG with the revisions in place. <u>Note:</u> You can revise your strategies and/or STGs at any point during the process.

Task Adapted From:

    Randall, L. (1992). <u>The student teachers' handbook for physical education.</u> Champaign, IL: Human Kinetics.

TASK 14
Student Success
Systematic Observation Worksheet

ST/PT _____   School _____
Date _____

<u>Application of Goal Setting Model</u>

<u>Step 1</u> – Identify Problem – gauging student success across skill levels and handicapping conditions

<u>Step 2</u> – Collect Baseline Data – the **CT/P** records the number of skill attempts and their success across a variety of skill/fitness levels or handicapping conditions. In order to complete this task, the **CT/PT** must complete the following steps:

    a.   select 4 students at low (precontrol or control), medium (utilization) and high (proficiency) skill levels as well as a student with special needs, and record their names at the appropriate category (by skill or SSN line) or students at different levels of fitness (low to high).

    b.   decide on what constitutes success (e.g., fitness activity – full participation, or if you monitor heart rates – exercising in the target heart rate zone; skill activity – maybe the **ST/PT** may focus on one or two skill components and that would define success for that day) or you may define success differently for the student with special needs (SSN)

    c.   during the skill and/or fitness activities record the number of skill attempts as well as the number of successful attempts

    f.   count attempts and successes of student in 1 or 2 minute intervals

    g.   calculate percent success rate and note of the total number of skill/fitness activity attempts

<u>Note 1</u>. The number of skill attempts (<u>across the same number of intervals completed</u>) and rates of success should be similar across skill levels and handicapping conditions.

<u>Note 2</u>. The **ST/PT** and **CT/P** must also decide how to handle skills with continuous movement (e.g., running, dribbling, etc.). A suggested strategy might recommend that the **CT/P** watch the skill for 5 seconds and then decide if the skill attempt was successful.

Baseline

List Criterion for Success: _____

OR

List Separate Criteria for Success for students' (Ss) skill/fitness level or handicapping condition:

Low- _____
Medium - _____
High - _____
SSN - _____

Low skill/fitness Ss _____   Medium skill/fitness Ss _____

1.		1.	
2.		2.	
3.		3.	
4.		4.	
5.		5.	

Total no. of attempts   _____   Total no. of attempts   _____
Total no. of successes _____   Total no. of successes _____
Percent successes   _____   Percent successes   _____

High skill/fitness Ss _____   Spec. Needs Ss _____

1.		1.	
2.		2.	
3.		3.	
4.		4.	
5.		5.	

Total no of attempts   _____   Total no. of attempts   _____
Total no. of successes _____   Total no. of successes _____
Percent Success   _____   Percent success   _____

Key = 1 (skill/fitness attempt) & x (successful skill/fitness attempt)

Step 3 – Set Specific a LTG and/ or Specific STGs – state these in observable terms
(e.g., percentage of successful students).

Note.   The LTG should reflect the Suggested **BTPS.**

LTG _____

STG #1_____

STG #2_____

STG #3_____

Step 4 – List Strategies to Help You Attain your LTG – See "Suggested Strategies" under
#4

1. _____
_____
_____
2. _____
_____
3. _____
_____
4. _____
_____
5. _____
_____

Step 5 – Collect data throughout week (3-4x elementary or 2-3x secondary level)

Class   #1   #2   #3   #4   (circle one)

List Criterion for Success: _____

OR

List Separate Criteria for Success at students' (Ss) skill/fitness level or handicapping condition:

          Low – _____

          Medium – _____

          High – _____

          SSN – _____

Low skill/fitness Ss _____   Medium skill/fitness Ss _____

1.	1.
2.	2.
3.	3.
4.	4.
5.	5.

Total no. of attempts _____   Total no. of attempts _____
Total no. of successes _____   Total no. of successes _____
Percent Success _____   Percent successes _____

High skill/fitness Ss _____   Spec. Needs Ss _____

1.	1.
2.	2.
3.	3.
4.	4.
5.	5.

Total no. of attempts _____   Total no. of attempts _____
Total no. of successes _____   Total no. of successes _____
Percent Success _____   Percent success _____

Key = 1 (skill/fitness attempt) & x (successful skill/fitness attempt)

Compare % to Your STGs & LTG:

List Goal(s) You Achieved _____

Make multiple copies of this page

Step 6 – Collect Post Test Data and Compare average to Your LTG

Post Test Class

List Criterion for Success: _____

OR

List Separate Criteria for Success for students' skill/fitness level or handicapping condition:

Low – _____

Medium – _____

High – _____

SSN – _____

Low skill/fitness Ss _____   Medium skill/fitness Ss _____

1.		1.
2.		2.
3.		3.
4.		4.
5.		5.

Total no. of attempts   _____   Total no. of attempts   _____
Total no. of successes   _____   Total no. of successes   _____
Percent Success   _____   Percent successes   _____

High skill/fitness Ss _____   Spec. Needs Ss _____

1.		1.
2.		2.
3.		3.
4.		4.
5.		5.

Total no. of attempts   _____   Total no. of attempts   _____
Total no. of successes   _____   Total no. of successes   _____
Percent Success   _____   Percent success   _____

Key = 1 (skill/fitness attempt) & x (successful skill/fitness attempt)

Compare Ave. Time to Your LTG:

Ave. Time _____   Achieved LTG – YES   or   NO (circle one)

Discuss your results: (for example: what strategies worked best, what goal difficulties did you encounter, or what did you learn)

_____

_____

_____

Step 7 – If you did not achieve your LTG – Review Strategies and/or STGs and continue to work. Please note that you can modify strategies or STGs at any point in this process.

Space provided for **ST/PT** to review Strategies and review goals (if needed):

_____

_____

_____

_____

References

References

Anderson, W.G., & Barrette, G.T. (Eds.). (1978). *What's going on in gym: Descriptive studies of physical education classes. Monograph 1 Motor Skills: Theory into Practice.* Champaign, IL: Human Kinetics.

Ashy, M., Lee, A., & Landin, D (1988). Relationship of practice using correct technique to achievement in a motor skill. *Journal of Teaching in Physical Education, 7 ,* 115-120.

Berliner, D. (1984). The half-full glass: A review of research on teaching. In P. Hosford (Ed.). *Using what we know about teaching.* (pp. 51-81). Alexandria, VA: Association for Supervision and Curriculum Development.

Berliner, D. (1987). Simple views of classroom teaching and a simple theory of classroom instruction. In D. Berliner & B. Rosenshine (Eds.), *Talks to teachers.* (pp. 93-110), New York: Random House.

Berryhill, L., & Jarman, B. (1979). *A history of lawsuits from physical education, intramurals and interscholastic athletics in the western United States: Their implications and consequences.* Provo, UT: Brigham Young University.

Block, M.E. (1994). *A teacher's guide to including students with disabilities into regular physical education.* Baltimore, MD: Paul H. Brookes Publishing.

Boyce, B.A. (1997). Inappropriate student behavior – A problem for student teachers. *Journal of Physical Education, Recreation and Dance, 68*(6), 29-30.

Boyce, B.A., & King, V. (1993). Goal setting for coaches. *Journal of Physical Education, Recreation and Dance, 64*(1), 65-68.

Brophy, J. (1983). Classroom organization and management. *The Elementary School Journal, 83,* 265-286.

Brophy, J. (1982, January). On praising effectively. *The Education Digest,* 16-19.

Brophy, J., & Good, T.L. (1986). Teacher behavior and student achievement. In M.C. Wittrock (Ed.). *Handbook of research on teaching* (3rd ed.). (pp. 328-391). New York: Macmillan.

Buck. M., Harrison, J. & Bryce, G. (1991). An analysis of learning trials and their relationship to achievement. *Journal of Teaching in Physical Education, 10,* 134-152.

Darst, P.W., & Pangrazi, R.P. (2002). *Dynamic physical education for secondary school students*. San Francisco, CA: Benjamin Cummings.

Doyle, W. (1979). Making managerial decisions in classrooms. In L. Duke (Ed.), *Classroom management (78th yearbook of the National Society for the Study of Education, Part, 2)*. Chicago: University of Chicago Press.

Fishman, S., & Toby, C. (1978). Augmented feedback. In W.G. Anderson & G.T. Barrette (Eds.), *What's going on in gym: Descriptive studies of physical education classes, Monograph 1 Motor Skills: Theory into practice*, (pp. 51-62). Champaign, IL: Human Kinetics.

Gage, N. (1984). What do we know about teaching effectiveness? *Phi Delta Kappan, 66(2)*, 87-93.

Goldberger, M., & Gerney, P. (1990). Effects of learner use of practice on skill acquisition. *Journal of Teaching in Physical Educaiton, 10,* 84-95.

Graham, G., Holt/Hale, S.A., & Parker, M. (2001). *Children moving: A reflective approach to teaching children physical education.* (5th ed.). Mountain View, CA: Mayfield.

Graham, G., Holt/Hale, S.A., & Parker, M. (1998). *Instructor's guide for children moving: A reflective approach to teaching children physical education.* (4th ed.). Mountain View, CA: Mayfield.

Graham, K.C., Hussey, K. Taylor, K. & Werner, P. (1993). A study of verbal presentation of three effective teachers. *Research Quarterly for Exercise and Sport, 64,* 87A (Abstract).

Harrison, J.M., Blakemore, C.L., & Buck, M.M. (2001). *Instructional strategies for secondary school physical education* (5th ed.). Boston: McGraw Hill.

Hellison, D. (1995). *Teaching responsibility through physical activity*. Champaign, IL: Human Kinetics.

Holt/Hale, S.A. (2001). *On the move: Lesson plans to accompany children moving* (5th ed.). Boston: McGraw-Hill.

Locke, E. A., & Latham, G. P. (1990). *A theory of goal setting and task performance.* Englewood Cliffs, NJ: Prentice Hall.

Magill, R.A. (1994). The influence of augmented feedback during skill learning depends on characteristics of the skill and learner. *Quest, 46,* 314-327.

Markos, N., & Boyce, B.A. (1999). What is your class management IQ? *Strategies, 12*(6), 13-15.

Medley, D. (1977). *Teacher competence and teacher effectiveness.* Washington, DC: American Association for Colleges of Teacher Education.

Merriman, J. (1993). Supervision in sport and physical activity. *Journal of Physical Education, Recreation and Dance, 64(2),* 20-23.

Metzler, M.W. (1989). A review of research on time in sports pedagogy. *Journal of Teaching in Physical Education. 8,* 87-103.

Metzler, M.W. (1990). *Instructional supervision for physical education.* Champaign, IL: Human Kinetics.

Mosston, M., & Ashworth, S. (1994). *Teaching physical education* (4thed.). New York: Macmillan College Publishing Company.

Owens, D., & Bunker, L.K. (1989). *Golf: Steps to success.* Champaign, IL: Leisure Press.

Pangrazi, R.P., & Dauer,V.P. (1995). *Dynamic physical education for elementary school.* Boston, MA: Allyn and Bacon.

Pangrazi, R.P., & Darst, P.W. (1997). *Dynamic physical education for secondary school students.* (3rd ed.). Boston, MA: Allyn and Bacon.

Randall, L. (1992). *The student teacher's handbook for physical education.* Champaign, IL: Human Kinetics.

Rink, J. (1985). *Teaching for learning in physical education.* St. Louis: C.V. Mosby.

Rink, J. (1993). *Teaching for learning in physical education.*(2nd ed.). St. Louis: C.V. Mosby.

Rink, J. (1996). Effective instruction in physical education. In Silverman & C. Ennis (Eds.). *Student learning in physical education: Applying research to enhance instruction* (pp. 171-198). Champaign, IL: Human Kinetics.

Rosenshine, B. (1983). Teaching functions in instructional programs. *Elementary School Journal, 27,* 61-64.

Schmidt, R.A. (1991). *Motor learning & performance: From principles to practice.* Champaign, IL: Human Kinetics Books.

Schmidt, R.A., & Wrisberg, R. (2000). *Motor learning and performance: A problem-based learning approach.* Champaign, IL: Human Kinetics.

Siedentop, D. (1983). *Developing teaching skills in physical education.* (2nd ed.). Palo Alto, CA: Mayfield Publishing Co.

Siedentop, D. (1991). *Developing teaching skills in physical education.* (3rd ed.). Mountain View, CA: Mayfield Publishing Co.

Siedentop, D., & Tannehill, D. (2000). *Developing teaching skills in physical education* (4th ed.). Mountain View, CA: Mayfield Publishing.

Siedentop, D., Tousignant, M. & Parker, M. (1982). *Academic learning time-Physical education: 1982 revision coding manual.* Columbus: School of Health, Physical Education, Recreation, Ohio State University.

Silverman, S. (1985). Relationship of engagement and practice trials to student achievement. *Journal of Teaching in Physical Education, 5,* 13-21.

Silverman, S. (1990). Linear and curvilinear relationship between student practice and achievement in physical education. *Journal of Teaching in Physical Education, 6,* 305-314.

Silverman, S., Devillier, R., & Ramirez, T. (1991). The validity of academic learning time – physical education (ALT-PE) as a process measure of student achievement. *Research Quarterly for Exercise and Sport, 62,* 319-325.

Soar, R.S., & Soar, R.M. (1979). Emotional climate and management. In P.l. Peterson & H.J. Walberg (Eds.). *Research on teaching: Concepts, findings & implications,* Berkeley, CA: McCutchen.

Stanley, S. (1977). *Physical education: A movement orientation.* (2nd ed.). New York: McGraw-Hill.

Swick, K.J. (1981). *Maintaining a productive student behavior.* Washington, DC: National Education Association.

U.S. Department of Health and Human Services (1996). *Physical activity and health: A report of the surgeon general.* Atlanta, GA: USDHHS, Centers for Disease Control and Prevention.

Viera, B.L., & Ferguson, B.J. (1989). *Volleyball: Steps to success.* Champaign, IL: Leisure Press.

Werner, P., & Rink, J. (1989). Case studies of teacher effectiveness in physical education. *Journal of Teaching in Physical Education, 4,* 280-297.

Wynne, E., & Ryan, K. (1997). *Reclaiming our schools: Teaching character, academics and discipline* (2nd ed.). Upper Saddle River NJ: Prentice Hall.

Yerg, B. (1978). Identifying teacher behavior correlates of student achievement. In *AAHPERD Research Consortium Symposium Papers: Teaching Behavior and Sport History* (Vol. 1, Book 1). Washington, DC: The American Alliance for Health, Physical Education, Recreation and Dance.